"Anyone looking for advice on embracing a more sustainable business model may not immediately turn to a book on marketing from an ex-chemicals executive. But it is precisely Clara Millard Dereudre's decades of experience and unique perspective that qualify her to reimagine the power of good marketing, and even in the most stubborn industries and environments. *Shifting the Marketing Mindset* is about rethinking the purpose of marketing to reconnect companies to the outside world, and to societies now yearning for a more hopeful future, with business leading the way."

Paul Polman, *Business Leader and Campaigner, Co-author,*
Net Positive: How Courageous Companies
Thrive by Giving More Than They Take

T0372481

Shifting the Marketing Mindset

A clarion call for marketing to return to its roots and integrate sustainability principles, this book illustrates how the marketing function can drive organizations, delighting customers and impacting positively on society and the environment.

Accused of manipulation and more, marketing is one of the most misused functions and misunderstood professions. The rise of "green marketing" could have been an opportunity for the profession to exhibit its potential to transform business—but instead, there has been a turn to greenwashing, with false claims of environmental friendliness. Now, businesses must evolve, rebalancing social and environmental priorities with economic ones, and it is time for a new era: Positive Impact Marketing. Drawing on almost 30 years of experience in global marketing, management, and strategy with private, public, and nonprofit organizations, this book introduces a framework organized around four key principles, **Connect 4 Impact,** and shows how these principles must govern marketing to achieve the desired net positive impact. It explains why and how marketing is key to establish sustainability at the core of business models and provides marketers with a toolkit and strategies for collaborating with other business leaders in the organization to guide rapid and effective transformations.

This book will be a transformative resource for leaders and managers looking to truly incorporate sustainability into their business models, marketing professionals at all levels, and MBA/BBA students with an interest in sustainable business.

Clara Millard Dereudre is a pragmatic visionary and seasoned leader with 25 years at Dow Chemical. Passionate about sustainable development, she held various leadership roles in sales, marketing, innovation, strategy, and sustainability. As a Sr Corporate Marketing Fellow, she integrated sustainability into business strategies. Appointed in 2021 as an Executive Director of Smart City at SIG, Industrial Services Geneva, she guides a sustainable and connected society. As a graduate of EDHEC and MBA holder, Clara teaches Sustainability Marketing and serves on various boards, advocating for businesses' role in society. She founded Greenbuzz Geneva to foster collaboration in sustainable development.

Shifting the Marketing Mindset

A Toolkit To Drive Sustainable Transformation

Clara Millard Dereudre

Routledge
Taylor & Francis Group

NEW YORK AND LONDON

Designed cover image: Getty

First published 2025
by Routledge
605 Third Avenue, New York, NY 10158

and by Routledge
4 Park Square, Milton Park, Abingdon, Oxon, OX14 4RN

Routledge is an imprint of the Taylor & Francis Group, an informa business

© 2025 Clara Millard Dereudre

ISBN: 978-1-032-72806-3 (hbk)
ISBN: 978-1-032-72803-2 (pbk)
ISBN: 978-1-003-42270-9 (ebk)

DOI: 10.4324/9781003422709

Typeset in Sabon
by MPS Limited, Dehradun

Contents

Foreword

In *Shifting the Marketing Mindset,* Clara Millard Dereudre offers us a much-needed **Connect 4 Impact** framework that can help both students and professional marketers transform marketing and make it lead player in the creation of a 21st-century sustainable world.

An honest look at the present-day world of business can only lead to the conclusion that we have not yet begun a major transformation to a sustainable economy. Yet, large companies have started to experiment with new solutions that promise a more sustainable economy, and thousands of start-ups are pushing us forward as well. With a long way to go for most of these initiatives to become truly sustainable, any communication about the sustainability efforts of businesses may easily be dismissed as greenwashing—and oftentimes rightly so.

Clara Millard Dereudre reminds us that marketing is not about communication only, but basically about understanding needs and finding ways to address those needs. Here is where marketing must start to reinvent itself to contribute to a sustainable future: Marketing should not only focus on the needs of consumers, but also the needs of all stakeholders—and especially, the needs of society and the planet. She also urges marketers to focus not only on present needs, but also on the needs of the future, and specifically the needs of future generations of stakeholders. This is a true paradigm shift for marketing—hence the name of her book, *Shifting the Marketing Mindset.* Attending to the needs of the planet and society, and the needs of the future is how marketers can make a transformative impact, and where the foundations are laid for more credible communication about business sustainability to consumers.

Business education is quickly evolving to prepare future leaders for an increasingly complex economy and society where the human goals of self-welfare and flourishing exist in symbiosis with planetary ecological systems. For this grander purpose of humanity, it will not be enough to add courses on corporate social responsibility or sustainability management and reporting to the curricula of business schools. This is, firstly, because a curriculum for future business leaders will need to put more emphasis on competencies such as systems thinking in order to deal with sustainability in all facets of a business—and beyond it in the social and ecological systems of which the business is a part. Secondly, systems thinking must find its way into the study of the typical disciplines of business such as operations, sourcing, finance, marketing, etc.

Exactly here is the place where *Shifting the Marketing Mindset* makes a great contribution. It invites marketers and students of marketing to understand the bigger picture of marketing itself, and its role in transforming businesses for a more sustainable economy. The book does not only offer the kind of conceptual frameworks that are needed in these unprecedented times, but also great examples and a personal touch through which the reader will obtain knowledge, develop skills, and become personally connected to sustainability marketing.

Tristan-Pierre Maury
Director of the Grande Ecole and Masters of
Sciences at EDHEC Business School
Bastiaan van der Linden
Director of the MSc in Global & Sustainable
Business at EDHEC Business School

Preface

Before exposing my beliefs about what the new marketing mindset needs to be, I would like to share more about how I came to believe in the huge opportunity, and dare I say, duty, we must bring about as leaders to ensure a greater tomorrow for our children and generations to come and how marketing can be instrumental in this transformation.

My first conviction concerns the role of business.

I was born in the early 1970s when consumerism was a sign of well-being and social success. The business mindset at the time, and consequently marketing, was focused on proposing the most appealing product or service to consumers and creating needs or rather "wants." For the enterprise, it was all about profit and for the consumers, the ability to acquire goods. I was able to study this phenomenon in business school and delve into why this was happening. At that time, the focus of teaching on business models was on how to increase profit in an ethical way. The influential, Nobel prize-winning economist, Milton Friedman, and his teachings on free-market capitalism were one of our main references. His familiar quote from 1970 says it all: "*There is one and only one social responsibility of business: to use its resources and engage in activities designed to increase its profits so long as it stays within the rules of the game, which is to say, engages in open and free competition without deception or fraud.*"

This stated role of business became rapidly uncomfortable for me, considering how I was raised in a rural environment, with profound consideration and true respect for natural resources and their limits. Secondly, my exposure to many countries, and developing countries, throughout my personal and professional path increased my awareness and sensitivity to the challenges of sustainable development. I believe that anyone who has had the opportunity to do business in developing countries such as those in Africa and parts of Asia becomes brutally aware of the challenges of resource management and inequalities. In Africa, where the population needs many basic resources, the people learn to respect those limited resources. How water and rainwater are managed is a good example of this. The principles of a circular economy come naturally, and the practices are well-honed. Every used item or material is considered a resource for another purpose. Not only is reduced consumption embraced but also the re-use of every resource ... by necessity. I remember meeting business leaders in Ethiopia, discussing ways to implement solutions to increase the circularity of raw materials in the expanding local textile industry. These leaders were adamant about a circular business model, and it was clearly in their DNA as they explained how a T-shirt, once it becomes worn and no longer usable as a piece of clothing, gets a third or fourth life as another purposeful material!

I witnessed during 25 years of my career in the chemical industry, an industry with a business model based on fossil fuels yet, as ironically as it may sound, with a mission that evolved to develop solutions to the world's most pressing challenges. Those challenges have evolved as we moved from the Industrial Revolution to consumerism and now sustainability. The chemical industry has supported the development of our society with access to sanitization solutions or medicines for example. It was a key accelerator to solutions required during the Industrial Revolution and brought a myriad of improvements and variety to existing products during consumerism. We indeed owe to the chemical industry most of what we are using every day. From the foam of our mattress or pillow to materials of our alarm clock, clean water or soap for our shower, cosmetics for our skin, building materials for our house, coating on the walls, tiles on the floor, food served at breakfast, spare parts of our car or bike, ... we could go on and on until the end of our day. Here is an industry one would not think of as being very sustainable, yet it has a great opportunity—as an industry—to bring solutions to many sustainability challenges. First, the chemical industry brings in solutions to improve health and nutrition. It can also play a key role in decreasing emissions for existing products or processes (e.g., water-based paints or inks), enabling recycling of materials (e.g., textiles or plastics), and better use of natural resources (e.g., water retention or water-saving solutions).

When I joined the agriculture sector of this industry, I saw another very tangible example of the challenges ahead. A rapidly growing global population and limited resources, requiring increased use of fossil fuel-based products to increase yield and meet food production needs, juxtaposed against increased pressure to develop solutions based on natural and renewable resources. This delicate balance made it crystal clear to me that the way of doing business and developing solutions must change. As a marketing and innovation professional as well as business manager, I realized we must change the paradigm of how we do business. If we are to solve the most pressing challenges facing current society, we must revisit traditional approaches of developing solutions based solely on our core business and direct partners. Sustainable development dictates that businesses consider the by-product of their activities, their externalities, from both an environmental and social perspective as well as on a time scale. It became clear that a company must operate in consideration for its many stakeholders beyond the direct ones that would include suppliers, customers or competitors, and government. I then felt the urge to join a business that would strive to strengthen bonds and partnerships with its stakeholders and in particular civil society and governments. When I later joined a public service company, it became clear how a business can create maximum positive impact on all its stakeholders and live by a mission to serve society and future generations. The value of public-private partnerships is already demonstrated to bring in sustainable solutions. Combining the respective strengths of these models certainly opens the way to the economic model and the role of businesses we need for tomorrow.

My second conviction concerns the opportunity of marketing.

Even as a professional in B2B marketing and business management for over 20 years and recognized as a Sr Global Corporate Marketing Fellow, a distinguished recognition for senior marketing professionals at Dow Chemical, it can be difficult to describe the real impact of marketing to those less exposed to it. I must admit I often felt dismayed about the image of marketing and how it was being performed in business. Originating from the primary sector of agriculture, driven by performance and cost without the luxury of partly or non-justified claims, I could argue that marketing helped develop solutions to improve value creation for its users, yet I could hear the skepticism of those wondering if most marketing efforts were simply aimed solely at increasing sales for the benefit of the company. That skepticism is here and rightly so because marketing has long been, and probably still is, primarily focused on driving sales, creating profits, and creating wants where there may be no real need. As a result, the perception of marketing today is one that is related to manipulation and consumerism, which obviously has a very bad press nowadays.

Yet such a perception, self-inflicted by marketing itself, ignores the core strength of marketing, which is to "connect the dots"—which means, to have a broader, systemic mindset, which makes marketing different from other functions in a company. For example, the production-related departments of a company are primarily focused on producing the company's product. The financial departments or functions of a company are primarily focused on managing the company's finances. While this is evolving for most functions, the marketing department, in contrast, has always been focused on building a relationship across the company and between the company and the world outside the company's walls. Marketing has always viewed the company and its capabilities or offerings as part of an ecosystem long before the term and even concept of "ecosystem" was developed in business.

And considering the sustainability challenges of today, connecting the dots among many stakeholders, and understanding the impact one can have on the other and how issues are interrelated—in other words, taking a systemic approach to address these challenges—is more vital than ever before. Systemic approaches are becoming critical firstly because the challenges are getting more complex and not so straightforward. The challenge to nourish a rapidly growing population with less arable land cannot easily be solved. Secondly because challenges are intertwined. It is impossible to work on one without impacting the other. Increasing food production has impacts on biodiversity, use of pesticides impacts climate change and soils, development of cities and growing urbanization limits arable lands, climate change impacts rural production cycles, reduced poverty gives access to meat for the poor which is also a source for further negative environmental impacts, etc. ... Sustainability requires to stop thinking and acting in silos but rather take a systemic approach. One that positions humans and nature in the center.

As an experienced marketer and business leader, I know the value marketing can create. Connecting the many dots is what our society and planet need today, and marketing, the pioneers of systemic thinking in the world of business, is best positioned to implement this approach. However, marketing needs to go back to its roots and be directed to value creation: Not delivering profits for a few shareholders but value for society and for the planet at large.

Realizing the notion of this opportunity of marketing to make a sustainable impact was an epiphany for me. I had already revisited how marketing and hence innovation could be redirected to address today's most pressing challenges. However, there was an opportunity to take this power of marketing to the next level of impact. I saw the need to apply a very strong systemic approach across the value chain, the local community, and the entire ecosystem.

All stakeholders in value chains as well as local and global ecosystems must be involved and aligned to the understanding of the impact—directly or indirectly, positive, or negative—on the other. This is certainly a new paradigm for business. And because many of the stakeholders, and typically the most impacted ones, are local, sustainability requires a local approach and consideration to challenges. This is where public service companies, such as telephone companies and electric companies, have their primary focus—one that global businesses need to integrate in their business model in order to be successful in their transformation.

This requirement for systemic approaches across all stakeholders, including the planet and with a strong consideration for local communities, is where marketing can be instrumental.

If it were not enough to be convinced as a practitioner, I also had the opportunity to thrash out this new role of marketing as a visiting professor teaching global marketing for sustainable business to MBA and MSc students, an audience quick to question and eager to see proof. My teaching experience reinforced my conviction of the role that marketing has to truly transform businesses and place sustainability at the core of the business models.

I call this opportunity for marketing to transform business: *Positive Impact Marketing.*

With this book, I hope to provide a toolkit for business leaders and marketers to drive and manage the sustainability transformation of their business model. I am convinced that marketing, which has long been criticized and misused, now has an opportunity to lead positive impact from businesses. With these new rules and mindset, marketing can be what business leaders missed to make the transformation of their business a reality, at its core and for the years to come.

This is a new era for marketing. One leading us to achieve our 2030 Sustainable Development Goals (SDGs) as well as reversing the trend of emissions, global warming, and increasing social imbalances.

Acknowledgments

I want to thank all my friends, colleagues, and sustainability leaders who have contributed, directly or indirectly, to this book. Leading sustainability in business is a long, and at sometimes a rather lonesome, process. A warm thank you to all the influential leaders that I have had the opportunity to meet along my path and who have fed my passion for the role of business in society.

I am grateful to those who provided me feedback as I was writing this book, Paul Polman for his support, and those who agreed to include their testimony thus bringing concrete cases: Jonathan Normand, Sascha Nick, Christian Brunier, Sabrina Cohen Dumani, Nicolas Freudiger, Bertrand Gacon, and last but not least Andrew Liveris.

A special thank you to Bastiaan van der Linden and Tristan-Pierre Maury for their nice foreword and providing me with the opportunity to teach sustainability marketing to EDHEC students.

I could not have written this book without the encouragement of my family, who supported me all along this writing exercise, and in particular my husband and two daughters, who have been patient with me as I spent hours behind my desk over weekends and vacations.

Finally, thank you to you, readers, who, in buying this book, demonstrate your willingness to act toward transforming our economic system and enable a sustainable development for all.

Introduction

Is marketing dead? Is this the end of an era? Accused of manipulation, one-way value creation, and accelerating consumerism by creating non-sustainable habits and wants, marketing is probably one of the most misused and misunderstood professions.

There are actually many definitions of marketing, one of the reasons being that it has evolved significantly together with our society and our economy. Marketing was once there to support production then sales and later on customers. Nowadays, the focus is switching to society. Marketing also takes on a different meaning depending on the company as well as the sector. For small to medium-sized companies, operational marketing seems to be predominant while a large multinational will typically look to have equal focus on the strategic and operational sides. Also, the focus differs on whether it's a business-to-business (B2B) or business-to-customer (B2C) model or depending on the type of product or service offered. We will then see a lower or greater focus on the different elements of marketing: communication, product development, and go-to-market to name a few.

Still today, most people think about communication when they hear about marketing. No surprise then that when thinking of marketing in a world where sustainability is more and more present, most think about greenwashing. And, unfortunately, many marketing and business practices are misusing the concepts of sustainability. The rise of "green marketing" or "sustainable marketing" could have brought forward a positive mission for marketing, an opportunity for the profession to exhibit its potential to transform business. Yet, we've seen instead a significant turn to green-washing with false claims of environmental friendliness.

Yet marketing has never had such an opportunity to impact and bring positive solutions for our future!

Today, I am excited to have the opportunity to teach MBA students in marketing for sustainable business as I truly believe marketing has a unique role to play in addressing the most pressing challenges of our

DOI: 10.4324/9781003422709-1

times. Today, if performed according to its original purpose and a mindset in step with the requirements for sustainable development, marketing *can* change the economic system and bring new sustainable economic models. As we reach the end of the post-industrial phase and new economic models emerge, marketing has this incredible opportunity, if not duty, to enable the necessary transformation of our economic model.

With challenges related to climate change and rising social inequalities, the role of business must evolve.

Many businesses have started transforming, looking to rebalance social and environmental priorities with economic ones. However, considering the urgency and consequences of the challenges, businesses must engage in deeper and more rapid transformations—revisit their purpose, and no longer take actions in isolation of the ecosystem around them. This is where marketing is the key player to drive the transformation of its organization.

We are starting to see more "social marketing" and "sustainable marketing" practices aimed at promoting responsible consumption and bringing forward "good" actions from companies. This trend has come with a negative effect: an increase in greenwashing. Green marketing has to some extent helped greenwashing expand. In most cases, so-called "sustainability initiatives" remain isolated and not connected between each other or in line with company strategy. The opportunity today is for marketing to lead companies and thus their products and services **and consumers** towards a positive impact.

This is a new era for marketing: the era of *Positive Impact Marketing*—where marketing drives positive impact for our society and environment, positioning business within its world.

Looking back at its original objective, the chief aim of marketing within an organization is to understand the market landscape and trends to bring solutions that meet the needs of the users. This is exactly what businesses must do today to have the impact on society that we need from them. Businesses need to better understand the ecosystem they operate in, their externalities, and how they can contribute to solving consumers' needs while considering social, environmental, and economic aspects equally. In this new paradigm, the role of marketing is to connect all these dots.

These are the new rules of the game toward Positive Impact Marketing!

The intent of this book is to help marketers and business leaders enable that paradigm shift and establish a new mindset for marketing. We will start by summarizing key sustainability fundamentals for businesses, showing why and how they need to evolve. This will be the opportunity to bring forward key concepts for sustainable development, starting with the definition of sustainability itself, as well as to define concepts that are central to sustainability transformations, that is, ecosystem, stakeholders, systemic approaches, or externalities. Those concepts are indeed central to operating a transformation toward sustainable business models. There are certainly a few more concepts within sustainability but the intent is to try to bring it down to the most fundamental ones for business leaders to successfully start and establish a transformation. These will be the concepts that will forge Positive Impact Marketing.

We will then look back at the evolution of marketing, highlighting the main pitfalls of greenwashing and defining the new rules for marketing. As the intent is to equip marketers with a methodology that will be easy to implement, these new rules will be regrouped into a methodology with four key elements. Because connecting the many dots is central to Positive Impact Marketing, I called that methodology: **Connect 4 Impact.**

These four key elements will be explained, and a toolkit will be proposed to Positive Impact Marketers. This toolkit will build on existing marketing tools that should be completed to integrate the key concepts of sustainability.

These four elements are a way to integrate key sustainability concepts into the marketing strategy:

- *Connect Stakeholders* where we will look at understanding the ecosystem and defining holistic stakeholders mapping to form impactful partnerships.
- *Connect Needs and Capabilities* where we will learn to focus on most pressing needs and strive to match those with existing or new capabilities, looking for complementarities and leveraging the power of collective intelligence.
- *Connect Beginning and Ends* where we will make a thorough impact assessment, define new business models to mitigate these impacts, or strive for net positive impact with a value proposition addressing financial, social, and environmental considerations, thus leading to a positive impact brand purpose.
- *Connect Say and Do* where we will make sure to fully and consistently operationalize the marketing strategy and create trust with the brand purpose.

Besides a proposed methodology, these elements represent a new mindset for marketing—one that is inspired by corporate social responsibility.

Finally, we'll highlight some of the key roadblocks to help leaders accelerate change.

The objective will not be to analyze these roadblocks in much depth as there is significant literature available on each of them. Instead, the purpose is to increase awareness of these to further strengthen the new marketing mindset proposed.

Chapter 1

The evolving role of business in society

Defining sustainability

Sustainability has become a buzzword ... used and misused by many. This has led to much confusion about what needs to be done, how it can be done, and by whom. I hence suggest starting with some definitions.

Published in 1987 by the World Commission on Environment and Development (WCED), the Brundtland Report, also called Our Common Future, defined the principles for sustainable development, creating the term that is commonly accepted today. "Our Common Future" was groundbreaking thinking in that it considered the environment and development as a single issue. It is especially noteworthy as it succeeded in placing environmental issues on the political agenda.

The Brundtland Report defined sustainable development as: "**development that meets the needs of the present without compromising the ability of future generations to meet their own needs.**"

The key principles proposed in this report towards a sustainable development are:

- An emphasis on **needs,** particularly of the global poor as well as opposed to wants or consumerism,
- **Equity** in distributing costs and benefits of growth,
- **Intergenerationality,** to consider long-term future needs,
- **Global environmentalism,** to understand the planet as a finite and vulnerable life support system.

This report laid the groundwork for the integration of economic, environmental, and social considerations and the concept of the three principles or pillars of sustainability: Profit, People, and Planet. This concept commonly, called the "3Ps," has evolved since and is also referred as the "triple bottom line," a phrase popularized by John Elkington in his book, *Cannibals with Forks: The Triple Bottom Line of 21st Century Business.*

DOI: 10.4324/9781003422709-2

 **Definition**

Sustainability: The ability to be maintained at a certain rate or level.
Sustainable development: Development that meets the needs of the present without compromising the ability of future generations to meet their own needs.
(Source: Bruntland Report and Investopedia)

A call for action: The genesis of sustainability

Over the last 50 years, we have seen increasing engagement from the international community on sustainability. With the first international conference on environment in Stockholm in 1972 through to the first Intergovernmental Panel on Climate Change (IPCC) report in 1992, awareness started to build on the challenges related to human activities and their impact on the planet and society. The Rio Declaration on Environment and Development, often shortened to the Rio Declaration, was a short document produced at the 1992 United Nations "Conference on Environment and Development" (UNCED), informally known as the Earth Summit. The Rio Declaration consisted of 27 principles intended to guide countries in future sustainable development. It was signed by over 175 countries. As a result, several global community efforts were launched aimed at raising awareness and seeking solutions for the challenges of sustainability. Key dates include:

- The Kyoto COP (Conference of Parties) in 1997, giving rise to the first international agreement on climate,
- The United Nations (UN) Millennium development goals in 2000 with eight international development goals for the year 2015,
- The Earth Summit in Johannesburg in 2002 with an agreement to focus on major threats to sustainable development and including substantial mention of multilateralism as the path forward,
- The ratification of the Kyoto protocol in 2005 committing nations to reduce greenhouse gas emissions,
- The RIO UN Conference on sustainable development in 2012 (Rio+20) gave rise to the non-binding document, "The Future We Want",
- The COP 18 in Doha in 2012 extended the life of the Kyoto Protocol,
- The COP 20 in Paris in 2015 led to the signature of the Paris Agreement and a commitment by signatories (196 parties to date) to reduce carbon

emissions and limit global warming to well below 2°C above pre-industrial levels and pursue efforts to limit the temperature increase to 1.5°C,
- The publication of the 17 UN SDGs (Sustainable Development Goals) that same year.

The scope of the SDGs issued by the United Nations in 2015 was unprecedented. The result of more than two years of consultation and stakeholder mapping, the SDGs provide a simple yet comprehensive roadmap for governments as well as businesses around the world. The 17 SDGs clearly explain the challenges and objectives for more sustainable development and are intended to be achieved by 2030. When they were issued, 193 countries agreed to these 17 SDGs.

The 17 SDGs can be categorized into three groups and visualized as a pyramid.

The base of the pyramid is known as the Earth System and consists of SDGs

15—Life on Land
14—Life Below Water
6—Clean Water and Sanitation
13—Climate Action

The second level of the pyramid, the Social System, consists of SDGs

1—No Poverty
11—Sustainable Cities and Communities
16—Peace, Justice, and Strong Institutions
7—Affordable and Clean Energy
3—Good Health and Well-Being
4—Quality Education
5—Gender Equality
2—Zero Hunger

The third level of the pyramid is the Economy System, which consists of SDGs

8—Decent Work and Economic Growth
9—Industry, Innovation, and Infrastructure
10—Reduced Inequalities
12—Responsible Consumption and Production

The top of the pyramid consists of SDG 17, Partnership for the Goals, and illustrates as such how these goals are usually interrelated as well as how partnerships can help accelerate the realization of each of these goals.

Unfortunately, despite these actions and increasing global coordination, the actions of the global communities and individual countries are still not up to the challenge. The year 2030 is rapidly approaching and we see increasing imbalances. The United Nations illustrates through their "alarming datapoints" the extent of the growing challenges we face from these increasing imbalances, as shown below (more information can be found on each imbalance and the reason for each goal under the United Nations website):

- Environmental imbalances include challenges such as biodiversity loss, waste management, resource scarcity, increasing pollution, heat waves, and climate change.

  - *Alarming datapoint: Earth Overshoot Day.* This marks the date when humanity has used all the biological resources that earth regenerates during the entire year. In 1970, this date occurred on December 31. It has steadily moved down ever since—to October in 1990, end of September in 1995 and end of August in 2004. In 2023, this day landed on August 2. To illustrate the impact of these changing dates, we needed 1 Earth to support humanity in 1970 but needed roughly 1.7 Earth in 2022.

- Social imbalances include challenges such as access to basic resources, inequalities and discrimination, education, health, safety and wellness, peace, justice, and human rights.

  - *Alarming datapoint*: in 2020, nearly one person in three lacked regular access to adequate food.

- Economic imbalances: externalities and wealth indicators, debts and liabilities, employment, financial markets, and real economy, influence of businesses.

  - *Alarming datapoint*: in 2020, one child in ten was engaged in child labor worldwide (160 million children).

And we could go on and on with illustrations of these imbalances. There are several publications available describing these imbalances, including the IPPC reports with its six assessments published from 2021 through 2023 or the Global Sustainable Development Report (GSDR) with its last edition published in 2023.

In the face of these pressing challenges becoming more and more visible, sustainability calls for a pursuit of new ways of producing, consuming, and living that protect the environment for the next generations.

Takeaway

With the exponential increase of environmental, social, and economic imbalances, despite the different initiatives at global and local levels, sustainability challenges are getting greater. This is an urgent **CALL FOR ACTION** for all of us.

The need for systemic approaches

In a summary of its Sixth Assessment Report on the state of climate change in the world issued in 2023, the UN's IPCC stated that it "recognizes the interdependence of climate, ecosystems and biodiversity, and human societies; the value of diverse forms of knowledge; and the close linkages between climate change adaptation, mitigation, ecosystem health, human well-being and sustainable development, and reflects the increasing diversity of actors involved in climate action."

This is a very clear and urgent call for action from all of us—the stakeholders. There are several different stakeholders and we'll come back with a more thorough approach later in the book. For now, let's look at three key groups: individuals, the public sector, and the private sector.

I personally believe that as inhabitants of this planet, individuals have a key role to play and, as such, should be placed at the center of considerations and actions. We are indeed the ones who vote and consume. As citizens, we influence politics with our choice of vote, and thus, the regulations that will support sustainable transformations. As consumers, we can influence both the economy and business models. I can decide to buy food or materials that are produced locally, or I can support the rising negative impact of international goods transportation, which represents a significant share of global emissions. In the end, if the consumer decides not to buy a product, a company must adjust its offering and hence its business model if it wants to survive. In this sense, the consumer is the most powerful of all stakeholders. For this reason, involving the inhabitant in the sustainability transformation is key. The good news is that we see more and more inhabitants aspiring to play an active role. It is now essential to equip them for that role by providing education and options.

The 2020 COVID-19 pandemic illustrates how with raising awareness and education of the population, sustainable behaviors can be adopted more rapidly. When travel was restricted, CO_2 emissions decreased, and we were made even more aware of the impact of emissions from cars or airplanes. This led the inhabitants to rethink their traditional transportation in favor of electric cars, public transportation, or biking. We have also seen scrutiny of the origin of products and a preference for locally sourced products when possible. Our sensitivity to consumption behaviors and habits and their impact on the planet has clearly increased. Yet there is only so much individuals can do either because they lack proper information or because solutions are not available at an affordable price. Making the right choice in a supermarket is not always possible, first because information is not easily available or sometimes misleading. For example, there are more and more misleading or incomplete labels being used on product packaging. For transportation, not everyone has all options at hand; taking public transportation or biking to work is not always possible. Finally, options might be available, but not always at an affordable price. The price of local food in Western developed countries, for example, is often higher than imported food that has traveled thousands of kilometers when one would expect the opposite.

Thus, even if very influential, the inhabitants alone cannot lead the sustainable transformation without the other stakeholders.

The public sector can play a tremendous role in accelerating the necessary evolution of the system. One way is using regulations or subsidies, which can be highly effective when supporting the scaling up of a specific technology. To that end, it should support solutions that are not yet competitive to give them an opportunity to reach maturity with scale. Renewable energy is a great example. By supporting the development and use of renewable energies, governmental departments and organizations can help these technologies scale and hence become competitive. The same goes for electric vehicles. Yet, regulations and public sector activities can work against the rules of the market. It can, for example, diminish competitive activities and individuals' ability to create innovative products or services. On the other hand, public organizations can also accelerate change by setting an example. For example, the public sector can show the way by choosing renewable energy solutions and local production for its own operations. While such commitments are essential, they will not suffice to prompt the necessary changes. To some extent, these public sector actions are not sustainable: because they are not self-funded, they do not strike the right balance between social and environmental considerations on the one hand and economic considerations on the other hand.

In order to balance social, environmental, and economic aspects, the private sector can offer the most sustainable solutions. It is the role of the private sector to offer sustainable solutions as it is in the very nature of business to offer solutions. In addition, it has the agility required to bring about innovations. In business, each challenge is an opportunity. Sustainability thus represents a huge opportunity for businesses. The Business and Sustainable Development Commission launched at the

World Economic Forum in Davos in January 2016 revealed its flagship report, "Better Business, Better World" (2017). This report shows that sustainable business models could open up economic opportunities worth at least US$12 trillion and up to 380 million jobs a year by 2030 in just four key economic areas (Energy US$4.3 trillion; Cities: US$3.7 trillion; Food and Agriculture US$2.3 trillion; Health and Well-Being US$1.8 trillion). This report involved more than 35 leaders from business, finance, civil society, labor, and international organizations.

Another consideration is the need for solutions to be intrinsically sustainable—which means solutions delivered by enterprises with business models that are self-sustaining over time. It's true that today, many positive impact solutions still require the support of grants or public funding. While this may be needed to scale solutions, as mentioned earlier, only when the business model is self-funding can these solutions be truly sustainable. This is the essence of sustainable development, which lies at the intersection of environmental, social, and economic needs.

It is clear that the role of the private sector is key to accelerate sustainable development. While businesses over the past few decades have created "wants," they now have an opportunity through the development of sustainable solutions to address needs, and thus act as a force for good. For this to happen, it is yet critical that the economic and financial system evolves. Key Performance Indicators (KPIs) for businesses should evolve from just economic to also environmental and social.

One could argue that there is a fourth key stakeholder: the Planet itself. Indeed, this is a major stakeholder for sustainability. Going further, it is the entire ecosystem that is a key stakeholder. The notion of ecosystem is central to sustainable development.

 **Definition**

Ecosystem: "An ecosystem or biome describes a single environment and every living (biotic) organism and non-living (abiotic) factor that is contained within it or characterizes it. An ecosystem embodies every aspect of a single habitat, including all interactions between its different elements." This term has given rise to the concept of **business ecosystem.**

(Source: biology dictionary)

As we can see in the previous paragraph, while there are several stakeholders, each being key, none of them can carry out the solutions needed on their own. It is only through the combined approach of all stakeholders that we will be able to address the challenge at hand.

With such interrelation among stakeholders, we can now understand how sustainability calls for systemic approaches. While the private sector provides the opportunity to significantly accelerate that transformation, it can only be successful by taking a systemic approach including other stakeholder groups and considering the ecosystem.

 Definition

Stakeholders: "Individual or group that has an interest in any decision or activity of an organization" (Source ISO 26000).

Systemic approach is "a way of studying and solving complex problems that cannot be reduced to simple parts." It involves "looking at the system as a whole and its interactions, structures, and emergent properties" (Source: afscet.asso.fr).

 Takeaway

There are many stakeholders contributing toward sustainable development. Those can be categorized into four key groups: individuals or inhabitants, the public sector, the private sector, without forgetting the planet or ecosystem. Yet none of them can have the entire impact needed on its own. Thus, as we look to establish sustainable transformations, it is key to take systemic approaches. The private sector can probably have the greatest impact but it is only through systemic approaches that deep sustainability transformations will happen.

Toward impact businesses

Evolving economic theories

American economist Howard Bowen introduced the concept of *social responsibility* of businesses with his book *Social Responsibilities of the*

Businessman (1953). It was the first comprehensive discussion of business ethics and social responsibility. It thus created a foundation for Corporate Social Responsibility (CSR). The concept of CSR recognizes that businesses have a responsibility to society beyond making a profit.

However, most of today's CEOs and business leaders were taught economic theories of free-market capitalism. The notion of the "invisible hand" introduced by the 18th-century Scottish philosopher and economist Adam Smith has served these theories. The idea behind the "invisible hand" is that letting everyone act in their own self-interests will lead to the best possible outcomes, socially as well as economically. In the 1970s, the economist Dr. Milton Friedman, who received the Nobel Prize in Economic sciences and was a strong advocate for free-market capitalism, claimed that "the sole responsibility of business is to increase profits for its shareholders"—an attitude that shaped the mindset of a generation of leaders and drove the design of business models in need of overhaul today.

It wasn't until nearly 20 years later that theories emerged with a different point of view, making the connection between sustainable development and corporate responsibility. We mentioned earlier the Brundtland Report or the Triple Bottom Line concept. More recently, the notion of *Shared Value* prompted a change in mindset and challenged the commonly accepted definition of capitalism.

Published in the *Harvard Business Review* in 2011, "Creating Shared Value" was an article written by Harvard Business School Professor Michael E. Porter and Mark Kramer, managing director of the social impact advisory firm FSG. They define shared value as "policies and operating practices that enhance the competitiveness of a company while simultaneously advancing the economic and social conditions in the communities in which it operates. Shared value creation focuses on identifying and expanding the connections between societal and economic progress."

The core idea here is that shared value must consider value created from both an economic and societal point of view. In their definition, they included environmental and social considerations within the societal realm. The notion of *shared value* differed significantly from prior economic theories until that time that focused solely on profit. Porter and Kramer's thinking was aligned with the trend toward embedding sustainability in business and looking at the three pillars of economic prosperity, environmental considerations, and social considerations.

This has reinforced the concept of the three principles or pillars (**The 3Ps**) of sustainable development: People, Planet, and Profits, looking for the intersection of these. It has also created greater awareness of the importance of stakeholders and externalities.

While these theories represented a significant change in traditional economic theories, they still position themselves from the perspective of the business. In that, they look at mitigating negative impacts and take a rather midterm approach. However, considering sustainability challenges, a paradigm shift is now needed. Businesses need to rethink their role in society and how they can operate within social and environmental boundaries. They also need to adopt a longer-term approach. We have then seen the emergence of a stronger focus on social and environmental concerns.

More recently, we started to hear about some theories that introduced the idea that the world and its resources are finite with biophysical resources as well as human and moral minimum standards to be respected. Economic models based on the principles of infinite resources cannot be sustainable as they benefit only part of the population with many being left aside. Latest economic models tend to position businesses at the service of the environment and society. They suggest a long-term focus for businesses becoming more responsible and looking to establish a happy society.

The evolution of economic theories is illustrated in Figure 1.1 where we see the economic, social, and environmental spheres and how each of these is positioned toward the other. While the economic sphere was still dominating the others in the early to mid-20th century, new economic theories advocate for the intersection of these spheres and the repositioning of business within social and environmental spheres.

There have been a few theories that supported environmental issues encompassing both social and economic issues, in particular Kate Raworth's theory of *doughnut economics*. First published as a report in Oxfam in 2012 and then further elaborated on in her book on Doughnut Economics in 2012, Raworth proposed a theory for the boundaries within which humanity (and hence businesses) must operate to meet the needs of all people within the planetary limits.

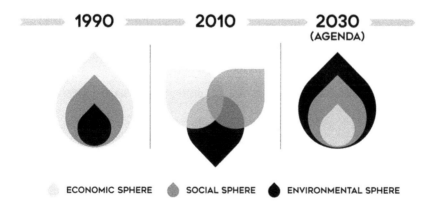

Figure 1.1 Evolving economic theories.

These limits are basically two concentric circles that resemble a doughnut. The inner circle represents the *social foundation* limit that ensures no shortfall of basic social needs such as energy, water, health, food, education, income and work, peace and justice, political voice, social equity, gender equality, housing, and networks. The outer circle represents the *ecological ceiling* limit, which guarantees no overshoot in environmental impacts such as ozone layer depletion, climate change, ocean acidification, chemical pollution, nitrogen and phosphorus loading, freshwater withdrawals, land conversion, biodiversity loss, and air pollution. The space in between the inner social foundation limit and the outer ecological ceiling limit represents the safe and just space for humanity to operate.

On August 19, 2019, the Business Roundtable, a group of more than 180 CEOs from America's largest companies, issued its latest statement on the purpose of a corporation:

"Businesses play a vital role in the economy by creating jobs, fostering innovation, and providing essential goods and services. Businesses make and sell consumer products; manufacture equipment and vehicles; support the national defense; grow and produce food; provide health care; generate and deliver energy; and offer financial, communications and other services that underpin economic growth. While each of our individual companies serves its own corporate purpose, we share a fundamental commitment to all our stakeholders".

Most recently, we have started to hear about *net positive companies*, a concept supported by Paul Polman and Andrew Winston. In short, the net positive economy represents the next step for business. That is, while businesses must mitigate their negative impact and act within boundaries, they have an opportunity, if not a duty, to look for ways to increase their positive impact (Figure 1.2). As such, businesses should look for more ambitious goals in order to have a net positive impact and hence regenerate the world. The idea is to multiply the positive impact for multiple stakeholders and not just a few as implied by most economic theories. These companies embrace purpose at the core of their strategy. They "create value from values".

As we can see, the social responsibility of business has been refined through the last century. Stakeholders have become central to the business strategy and their commitment has become critical. With the greater focus on stakeholders came forward the idea of externalities—the external impact of the company's activities. What are the direct and indirect impacts a company has on its ecosystem? This concept of externalities has become central to the concept of sustainability and the

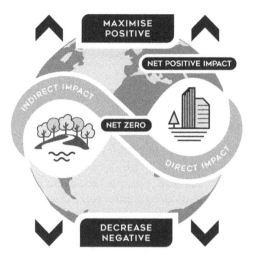

Figure 1.2 Net positive impact.

role of business in society. It aims at repositioning the business and the company in its world. We'll come back to externalities when we discuss the implications of externalities for marketing.

 Definition

Externalities: An externality is a cost or benefit caused by a producer that is not financially incurred or received by that producer. An externality can be positive or negative and can stem from either the production or consumption of a good or service. The costs and benefits can be both private—to an individual or an organization—or social, meaning it can affect society as a whole.

(Source: Investopedia)

Takeaway

Economic theories have significantly evolved since the beginning of the 20th century. Businesses can no longer operate in isolation and being mainly driven by profit. Responsible companies will consider their stakeholders and the ecosystem they operate in, and respect planetary boundaries and social fundamentals. The concept of externalities and how to manage direct and indirect impacts of the business on their ecosystem and stakeholders becomes central to the most recent economic theories looking to support a sustainable development.

The spectrum of organizations

The growing awareness of externalities of businesses leads to new ways to categorize organizations. A spectrum of organizations can be drawn, ranging from those seeking to achieve positive social/environmental impact to those guided purely by market/economic rules (Figure 1.3).

On one side of this spectrum, we find *non-profit organizations*. These are critical to our society. They help address inequalities, access to basic needs, or initiate trends. Yet these organizations can exist only if supported by government, the private sector, or individuals. Grant-based organizations are not by definition self-sustainable. Moving along the spectrum, we see more *social enterprises*. Some are non-profit and others looking to extract profit. These struggle to find scale mainly because they lack a focus on profit that would enable them to invest and grow. Many social entrepreneurs are driven by social and environmental impact and consider profit to be "evil." For that reason, their positive impact can only be limited in scope and time, and they struggle to become high-impact businesses.

Impact businesses are those still too rare enterprises that manage to be driven by social and environmental impact yet extract enough profit to fund their growth, increase their impact, and become high-net positive impact businesses.

Further to the right, in the for-profit section of the spectrum, are *sustainable business* companies taking steps to reduce their carbon footprint or negative social impact where they operate. CSR has become

Figure 1.3 The spectrum of organizations.

a must for many companies. However, CSR is in many cases still an activity done to the side of the core business. Many of these companies are now setting carbon reduction targets for themselves. As such, they are looking to decrease and often compensate for their negative footprint. We now see these companies engaging in carbon offset programs. They monitor the impact of their emissions on their operations and value chains. These companies are also looking to have a more inspiring mission or purpose aligned to sustainability challenges. This is certainly very encouraging.

However, we still see too many disconnects between claims and real net impact. One typical gap is when these companies look at their products or services in isolation from their entire life cycle (e.g., what happens to the product after it is no longer used?) or the externalities of the company (e.g., what is the impact of transporting the product?). Considering the challenge ahead and the urgency to reverse the trend on climate change, can these actions suffice? By integrating social and environmental drivers or filters into their activities, these companies can become high-impact businesses (i.e., moving to the left on the spectrum). Becoming an impact business implies that CSR is no longer just an activity on the side but rather truly embedded in all the company is doing and its strategy.

As pointed out again in the latest IPCC report, the effect of human activities on climate change is now proven. This is our entire economic system that is in question. We have reached the end of an economic model mainly based on producing more, selling more, and making more profit—a system that is very linear: produce—use—dispose. Here is an opportunity for businesses to redefine who they are based on their role in society and looking at their holistic environmental and social footprint. It is not just about having an inspiring mission or purpose. The opportunity is to define business models around that mission—that is, putting that mission at the core and embedding in that mission all the company is doing as well as its externalities. It is about placing sustainability at the core of the business strategy and all activities emanating from that strategy. As explained earlier, it is about operating within planetary boundaries and social fundamentals. Those businesses able to balance social, environmental, and economic impact and play at that intersection have earned entry into the category of impact businesses.

This new approach to business involves a new economic system. One that rewards not just a good product but rather good companies. One where companies are balancing their search for profit with a commitment toward their impact on society and the environment. It goes further than this. In this new economic system, businesses are driven toward maximizing positive impact and decreasing negative impact on their environment and on society while creating the value and profit needed to sustain this value creation. This is a paradigm change where profit is made from addressing sustainability challenges and in full consideration of these. We are moving from a system driven by shareholders to one focused on stakeholder value. The shareholder system focuses on profit and a handful of stakeholders. Cost and short-term impacts are given more consideration than externalities. In contrast, stakeholder models are focused on externalities, optimizing positive impact on stakeholders whether they are employees, the community, society, or the environment in which it operates.

Thus, for businesses to become impact businesses, it is critical that they understand their externalities—the impact they have on the environment and on society. They need to engage with their stakeholders along the whole value chain and life cycle of their product; develop solutions that matter for society and address the most pressing challenges of our society; and influence stakeholders to engage in the right behaviors.

This is where marketing has a key role to play. While marketing is more associated with outward communication, it is also the DNA of marketing to understand the environment, define solutions, and develop business models that create value, aligning strategy and action. Marketing, in its very nature, can drive the evolution of businesses as we need it. Going back to its "raison d'être," marketing can lead the transformation of businesses toward impact businesses, heralding a new era of *Positive Impact Marketing*.

 Takeaway

The role of business in society is evolving. While there are still different types of businesses, sustainability calls for positive impact businesses. Those businesses have built their business models toward optimizing positive impact in consideration of planetary boundaries and fundamental social needs. These businesses operate in their world with a deep focus on their externalities. Positive Impact Marketing, going back to its roots linked to environmental analyses, is the opportunity to **help establish positive impact business models.**

A new toolkit for businesses

With the evolving role of business in society, we have seen a new set of tools being made available to help businesses in their transformation. I would like to highlight two major initiatives that provide a new compass for businesses.

The call of the UN to businesses

The SDGs described earlier in this chapter are being used more and more by companies to set their sustainability transformation roadmap. In parallel to the 17 SDGs, the United Nations Global Compact, founded in 2000, proposed a simple, universal, and voluntary framework of commitment, based on ten principles grouped into four categories—Human Rights, Labor, Environment, Anti-corruption—as follows (source: United Nationals Global Compact website):

Human rights

Principle 1: Businesses should support and respect the protection of internationally proclaimed human rights; and
Principle 2: make sure that they are not complicit in human rights abuses.

Labor

Principle 3: Businesses should uphold the freedom of association and the effective recognition of the right to collective bargaining;
Principle 4: the elimination of all forms of forced and compulsory labor;
Principle 5: the effective abolition of child labor; and
Principle 6: the elimination of discrimination in respect of employment and occupation.

Environment

Principle 7: Businesses should support a precautionary approach to environmental challenges;
Principle 8: undertake initiatives to promote greater environmental responsibility; and
Principle 9: encourage the development and diffusion of environmentally friendly technologies.

Anti-corruption

Principle 10: Businesses should work against corruption in all its forms, including extortion and bribery.

The 17 SDGs are linked to the ten principles, with each SDG addressing a minimum of two principles—for example, SDG 4 Quality Education addresses the two principles of human rights. Grouping the SDGs into four categories and ten key principles provides a simplified way for businesses to think about their sustainability impact and strategies.

The International Organization for Standardization (ISO) 26000 initiative

The ISO 26000 norm deals with the social responsibility of businesses. Unlike all other ISO norms, it doesn't lead to a certification but is rather a roadmap for companies towards improved "societal" responsibility, i.e., social and environmental. The purpose of the norm is to create a harmonized approach across countries and a comprehensive toolkit. This project, initiated in 2001, involved over 500 experts from 99 countries, was published in 2010, and represents the beginning of a structured approach to social responsibility for companies.

This standard defines social responsibility as the "responsibility of an organization for the impacts of its decisions and activities on society and the environment, through transparent and ethical behavior that:

- Contributes to sustainable development, including health and the welfare of society,
- Considers the expectations of stakeholders,
- Follows applicable law and consistent with international norms of behavior,
- Is integrated throughout the organization and practiced in its relationships."

ISO 26000 covers seven core subjects, thus taking a holistic approach and highlighting interdependencies. The seven core subjects cover all aspects of an organization from *human rights, community involvement and development,* and *labor practices* to *fair operating practices, consumer issues,* and the *environment,* all centered around *organizational governance.*

As explained earlier, one of the fundamental concepts central to sustainable development is the notion of externalities. The ISO 26000 framework provides a very complete toolkit for companies to identify their direct impact as well as their indirect impact on the environment or stakeholders. Some of these tools will be further explained later in the book.

In parallel and complementary to these initiatives are initiatives that aim at providing tools for businesses to assess their impact and thus develop strategies for mitigating negative impact as well as optimizing positive impact. B Lab, a non-profit organization founded in 2006, is another such initiative seeking to transform the global economy to benefit all people, communities, and the planet. It aims to support the environmental and social impact assessment of companies. When companies have mitigated their impacts, put plans in place, and followed through for further improvements, they will receive a company certification issued by B Lab known as "Benefit Corporation" or "B Corp." Another initiative focused on environmental impacts is CDP, a not-for-profit charity founded in 2000, that runs the global disclosure system for investors, companies, cities, states, and regions.

 Takeaway

Tools are available to support businesses in establishing their CSR strategies and their sustainability transformation. These frameworks are very powerful to help redefine business models and establish businesses that have a positive impact on society and the environment.

 Testimony

Acting toward a "benefit for all" economic system

Jonathan Normand—Founder and CEO at B Lab (Switzerland) Foundation

A world battling to respond to a sustainability crisis that threatens its long-term existence can only find solutions through a united effort in which actors from all domains interact and work together. Individual concerns and interests must be replaced by shared goals. Thus, in our economic system, all stakeholders touched by economic activity must work together: from citizens to investors, from activists to policymakers, and from consumers to academic researchers.

For companies, this holistic stakeholder approach leaves behind the profit-oriented mindset exemplified by Milton Friedman's shareholderism—which argues the only purpose of a business is to create profits for shareholders—to stakeholderism, in which the purpose of a business is to ensure prosperity and perennity of all stakeholders.

B Lab, a non-profit organization, is working to release companies from the iron grip of shareholderism and instead move them to embrace the actions and mindset of stakeholderism. B Lap achieves this goal through the rigorous B Corporation (or B Corp) certification process that requires companies to prove that they have fully embraced stakeholderism—that is, they are driven by a business purpose that is not solely focused on profits but rather is science-based and regenerative and promotes human life and nature on the planet.

Thus, the "B" in "B Corp" stands for "benefit for all." Success is measured not by a single bottom line of profit but by a quadruple bottom line that builds on the triple bottom line of *people*, *planet*, and *profit* and adds a fourth P: *purpose*. Companies that receive the coveted B Corp badge have shown that they fully incorporate into their purpose the needs and welfare of society, and of the planet itself. They are driven by the desire to create an **inclusive, equitable,** and **regenerative economy** that benefits all.

To assess and verify that a company is indeed a force for good, we use a standard tool known as the B Impact Assessment (BIA). This provides a comprehensive framework through which companies can evaluate both their positive and negative impacts. In addition, they should also adapt their bylaws to reflect consideration for stakeholders and the planet. Subsequently, their results and scores are published transparently on the Public B Corp Directory.

B Corps certification is not a one-off; every three years, B Corps must be recertified, thus ensuring that the company is continuously improving its sustainability efforts.

The B Corp badge, however, is only the beginning. We want to lead the way to fundamentally change the economic ecosystem on our planet, which means not only changing the behavior and culture of companies but also changing the structural underpinnings of the capitalist system. In short, our goal is to build a "purpose ecosystem." Since our founding in 2006, we have also collaborated at local, national, and regional levels with governmental bodies and policymakers; private sector, civil society, and NGO organizations; and academic institutions. We have participated in multiple initiatives and alliances, in which we exchange insights, innovative practices, and advocate for change through building public awareness and promoting new policies.

B Corp represents a transformative movement, transcending mere certification to embody a commitment to using collaboration and collective action for economic and societal ecosystem transformation. This shift aims to replace traditional models of extraction and waste with principles of regeneration and long-term sustainability, a change we believe is crucial for the future of our planet.

At the heart of this movement is the B Lab network, a pioneering force in global economic systems change. Our network sets the standards, devises policies, and develops tools and programs that guide businesses toward more sustainable and ethical practices. Central to our mission is the certification of companies as B Corps, signifying their leadership in this transformative journey.

Our community is expansive, encompassing over 600,000 workers in more than 8,500 B Corps across 80 countries and 150 industries. Additionally, over 300,000 companies utilize our B Impact Assessment and the SDG Action Manager to measure and manage their impact.

B Lab's influence extends to legal reform, having spearheaded the creation and passage of over 50 corporate legal statutes globally. These statutes enable stakeholder governance, a paradigm shift embraced by over 25,000 companies through our legal framework. Together, we are not just reimagining business; we are actively rebuilding it to benefit all people, communities, and the planet.

Conclusion

Since the first IPCC report in 1992, there has been undeniable evidence for the case for change and a clear call to action. All stakeholders have a key role to play individually as well as uniting in adopting a systemic approach towards sustainability. One of these stakeholders is the economic sector. Businesses have a new role in society. Sustainability will thus require a new mindset for businesses. They can no longer operate in isolation driven by a single-minded quest for profit. Identifying and understanding their impacts on their stakeholders and the ecosystem they operate in is fundamental. Only businesses that look to maximize their positive impact and position that objective at the core of their business model will become the positive impact businesses we need. CSR tools made available by organizations such as the UN or ISO will be essential for business leaders to implement these transformations.

Bibliography

Better Business, Better World, Report. Business and Sustainable Development Commission—United Nations, 2017.

Creating Shared Value. An article written by Harvard Business School Professor Michael E. Porter and Mark Kramer. *Harvard Business Review*, 2011.

Earth Overshoot Day Research Report. https://www.overshootday.org/content/uploads/2022/06/Earth-Overshoot-Day-2022-Nowcast-Report.pdf

Global Sustainable Development Report (GSDR). https://sdgs.un.org/gsdr, 2023.

Howard R. Bowen. *Social Responsibilities of the Businessman.* Harper, 1953.

IPCC_ Intergovernmental Panel on Climate Change Report. https://www.ipcc.ch/report/sixth-assessment-report-cycle, 2023.

John Elkington. *Cannibals with Forks: The Triple Bottom Line of 21st Century Business.* John Wiley and Sons Ltd, 1999.

Kate Raworth. *Doughnut Economics. Seven Ways to Think Like a 21st-Century Economist.* Random House Business, 2018.

Our Common Future. *The World Commission on Environment and Development— United Nations.* Oxford University Press, 1987.

Paul Polman and Andrew Winston. *Net Positive. How Courageous Companies Thrive by Giving More Than They Take.* Harvard Business Review Press, 2021.

Social Responsibility. Discovering ISO2600. https://www.iso.org/publication/PUB100258.html, 2010.

The Systemic Approach: What Is It All About? Association Française de Science des Systèmes (afscet), 2003.

Chapter 2

A new era for marketing

To understand the new era of marketing, we begin by clarifying the definitions of three types of marketing, which reflect the evolution of marketing in recent years in response to the growing awareness of sustainability issues.

Marketing definitions

Traditional marketing

The Chartered Institute of Marketing (CIM) defines marketing as "… the management process responsible for identifying, anticipating, and satisfying customer requirements profitably."

This seems like a fundamental part of what every business needs to do. As such, marketing is instrumental for businesses to increase their revenue and their profit. While the intention with this definition was to move away from a pure "inside-out" approach, this has, however, not alleviated the common negative perception of marketing. The function of marketing has been seen to favor the creation of wants and consumerism.

In 2017, the American Marketing Association (AMA) proposed a new definition for marketing: "Marketing is the activity, set of institutions, and processes for creating, communicating, delivering, and exchanging offerings that have value for customers, clients, partners, and society at large."

This definition brings a stronger focus on value to different stakeholders starting with the customers but also including partners and society at large. It proposes a stronger and broader "outside-in" focus to marketing.

Social marketing

In parallel to the evolving definitions and practices of marketing, we have seen the rise of social marketing.

DOI: 10.4324/9781003422709-3

While there are a few definitions for social marketing, it is essentially an approach used to develop activities aimed at changing or maintaining people's behavior for the benefit of individuals and society. Social marketing uses marketing methods combined with social sciences to change behaviors with the aim to increase social good.

For example, a campaign against tobacco or toward eating less fat would use a social marketing approach.

Green marketing

With the rise of sustainability challenges, we are seeing more green marketing initiatives. In plain English, green marketing refers to selling products or services by promoting their environmental benefits. It is also known as eco-marketing, environmental marketing, or societal marketing.

The reasons green marketing would be used include:

- to support the implementation of sustainable business practices,
- to demonstrate a company's social responsibility,
- to demonstrate the safe and purposeful nature of the product or service,
- to reduce expenses (packaging, transportation, energy/water usage, etc. ...).

There are many traditional ways green marketing can be implemented when a brand launches an environmentally friendly product: the product itself is eco-friendly; the packaging or lack thereof is designed to give this image; the product is recyclable and/or reusable, produced using green energy, or created from recycled materials to reduce waste; a local selling outlet used to reduce transportation energy; and more.

As a part of green marketing, brands also often participate in recycling programs. They become more scrupulous about waste disposal practices, donate to different green movements, and educate their customers on what they can do to protect the environment and why it matters.

So, over the years, we have seen an evolution of marketing in its orientation and focus. The focus has evolved from a focus on production (what can we make or do best?) to a focus on sales (how can we sell more aggressively?) to a focus on market: what do customers want and need? More recently, marketing has moved to a societal focus: what do customers want and need and how does what they want and need benefit society? (Figure 2.1)

Figure 2.1 The evolution of marketing.

⊞ Takeaway

The definition and role of marketing have significantly evolved since the beginning of the 20th century. In parallel to rising sustainability awareness, we have clearly seen an evolution toward an increased focus on stakeholders' value by marketing: customers, partners, and society at large.

The growing curse of greenwashing

For all its good intentions, green marketing has prompted the rise of greenwashing. Here are some of the more negative examples of green-washing we've seen emerge.

Selling part of the story

With green marketing, a company doesn't always tell the whole truth about a product or service but rather brings forward some specific green aspects without considering the entire footprint of a product on its whole life cycle. For example, if a product uses a new ingredient that is perceived as "greener" because of its natural aspect, it is important to consider the implication of the new ingredient on the footprint of the entire value chain. Perhaps the ingredient is sourced from the other side of the planet or through socially unacceptable practices such as child labor.

Creating new wants

Green marketing is not always looking to shift the consumer toward responsible consumption. Still today, in many cases, sustainable or green marketing is aimed at creating wants and does not address sustainability-driven needs. It instead promotes more consumption. For example, promoting the fact that a product is made from recyclable materials doesn't mean an increase in consumption won't have a negative impact on resources and emissions involved in its production and hence use. The fashion industry provides a good illustration. While we see more and more focus on the recycling of clothes, there are limited initiatives to reduce consumption, and fast fashion, which bases its business model on the frequent renewal of clothes, is still a common practice in the fashion sector. Patagonia, with its full-page ad in the 2011 Black Friday edition of the *New York Times* "Don't Buy This Jacket" addressed this issue.

Misleading the customer

We see many green marketing initiatives using noncertified labels thus misleading the consumer. Many companies are now even introducing their own labels. While there are recognized certifications, there has been an exponential increase of private labels which, in most cases, do not consider the entire life cycle of a product. One just needs to look on supermarket shelves to realize how many of these noncertified labels or unproven statements are used on packaging.

Inconsistencies with the company strategy

Finally, still too many green marketing activities are disconnected from the overall practices of the company. A company might launch a product or service perceived as green for its positive impact on the environment while in parallel, that company is doing very little to mitigate its overall footprint and improve its social responsibility. Obviously, as we are dealing with a transformation, one must accept that actions are taken one at a time, and change cannot happen overnight. If that is understandable, it's critical to be consistent across the enterprise on the approach and commitment to sustainability. What counts is that each individual activity in support of sustainability is consistent with other activities and in line with the overall company strategy for sustainability. This is critical to establish credibility and trust.

These major considerations provide some hints on how to avoid the trap of greenwashing—steps that will also be integrated into the new rules of marketing.

 **Definition**

Greenwashing: Using apparent pro-environmental activities to disguise the actual negative impact of a company's products and operations.

Takeaway

With the rise of green marketing, the marketing function, despite recent efforts to increase its focus on society at large, is at risk of falling again into the trap of manipulation. This has been given a name that is already famous: greenwashing.

Toward Positive Impact Marketing

Sustainability or sustainable marketing

Beyond green marketing, we also hear about "sustainability marketing" or "sustainable marketing." This typically takes on a more holistic approach. As such, it is closer to the definition of sustainability described in the Brundtland Report discussed in the first chapter.

Let's come back to the definition of sustainable development from the Brundtland Report (1987): "development that meets the needs of the present without compromising the ability of future generations to meet their own needs."

Sustainability or sustainable marketing will hence look at meeting the **"needs of the present"** ...

It is clearly the role of marketing to understand markets, trends, consumer needs, and most importantly unmet needs. When it comes to sustainability, we are not looking to create wants and support consumerism but rather to understand what the true unmet needs are to serve our planet and society.

Once those unmet needs are identified, it is the role of marketing to identify which capabilities can help address those needs and connect unmet needs with these. This is clearly aligned to the definition of traditional marketing described earlier ... **"without compromising the ability of future generations to meet their own needs."**

However, to bring sustainable solutions and advance sustainability, marketing must look not only for unmet needs to serve our planet and society but also for comprehensive solutions, taking into consideration the needs of future generations. That implies taking into consideration possible adjacent impacts, or externalities, on both the environment and society today as well as tomorrow.

That means that marketing will have to understand all externalities of a product or service, taking a very broad approach to the market and impact in space, time, and from a human perspective.

Sustainability marketing thus brings forward the importance of understanding the impact of a product or service on the environment and stakeholders, both directly and indirectly. It takes into consideration that impact all along the entire value chain and through the life cycle of the product.

Sustainability marketing is about how marketing principles can be used to address sustainability challenges, taking a holistic approach required for sustainability.

Here are a few guiding principles for sustainability marketing:

- We no longer look just at a product or service in isolation but include its impact on society and the environment today and in the future,
- We no longer look at the product in a linear way but rather over the entire life cycle of the product and make it easier for the consumer to positively impact this life cycle through recycling, reusing, and reducing,
- We no longer look just at the product but rather at the solution that will meet these unmet needs toward sustainable outcomes for all stakeholders,
- We no longer try to "fool" the consumer with labels or incomplete information but create trust in the products, services, and the company that provides these. We hence hear more and more about the need for marketing ethics.

This means a totally new mindset for marketing which can be summarized in Figure 2.2.

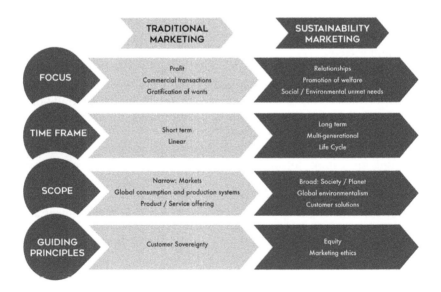

Figure 2.2 The evolution of the marketing mindset.

Sustainability marketing could be described as: "Planning, organizing, implementing, and controlling marketing resources and programs to develop customer solutions, while considering social and environmental criteria and meeting corporate objectives."

This definition brings forward the comprehensive role of marketing that also includes measurement and tracking aspects. It emphasizes the need for solutions for the end user that take into consideration social and environmental aspects. And finally, it highlights the necessity to ensure alignment with company objectives.

Referring to the earlier section, sustainability marketing will not lead to greenwashing thanks to the holistic approach with stakeholders, the thorough consideration of externalities, the transparency across the life cycle, and consistency with company strategy.

However, there is an opportunity for marketers to make a positive impact even beyond sustainability marketing. That opportunity is to help businesses become true and scalable impact businesses, with sustainable business models, and thus support the transformation of our economic system.

Transformational marketing

As explained earlier in the book, sustainability demands a paradigm shift and thus new economic systems. After decades of marketing being mistrusted, perceived as manipulative, and purely profit-driven, marketing now has a commendable opportunity. The opportunity being to create new business models and help establish positive impact businesses. I refer to this aptly as *Positive Impact Marketing*.

While sustainability marketing brings solutions to the most pressing needs (as opposed to creating wants) and seeks to mitigate the negative impacts of a business, Positive Impact Marketing looks at not only scaling these solutions but leading a deep transformation of our business models toward net positive impact business models. The opportunity for Positive Impact Marketing is to bring forward new sustainable economic models.

- For small social enterprises focused on people or planet, Positive Impact Marketing will help extract the profit needed to increase the positive impact of the enterprise through scale and over time, looking at the entire business model,
- For large businesses highly focused on profit but also working to transform themselves to reduce their negative environmental or social footprint, Positive Impact Marketing will take that transformation to the next level by truly embedding sustainability in the company strategy, placing sustainability at the core of its business model in order to target net positive impact.

Because impact businesses are all about having a positive social and environmental footprint and managing externalities today and tomorrow, Positive Impact Marketing requires placing the company in its world and over time. Positive Impact Marketing will help identify and create bridges between the needs of all stakeholders, employees, customers, suppliers, rivals, intermediaries, investors, communities, interest groups, government, media, and public-sector organizations. Positive Impact Marketing will also integrate all market trends including technology, politics, culture, and economics. Finally, Positive Impact Marketing must connect each product or service to the company mission and strategy (Figure 2.3).

This means the end of a linear or narrow approach and embracing instead a systemic one. With a systemic approach, marketing can be a key means to bring together the 3Ps of sustainable development: People, Planet, and Profit, and thus accelerate the positive impact of business.

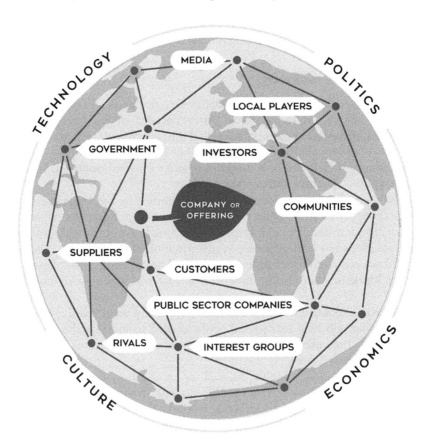

Figure 2.3 Transformational marketing.

Because connecting the dots is the very essence of marketing, marketing can best foster the systemic approaches needed to transform our economic system. While at the same time, marketing must help establish credibility through consistency of words and actions, claims and measurements, objectives, and impact. These tools are within the scope of marketing and need only be tapped.

In sum, the real opportunity for Positive Impact Marketing is to use the tools of marketing with renewed purpose and broader scope to enable a deep transformation of business models and companies and by doing so, create positive impact businesses. Positive Impact Marketing is the key to driving the sustainable transformation needed for our economic system.

Positive Impact Marketing represents first and foremost a new mindset for marketing, which is summarized in the box below and will be explored further in the upcoming chapters.

 Key steps

A new mindset for marketing

- Forge a sustainability mindset and develop an understanding of why and how the role of business needs to evolve toward positive impact businesses,
- Get familiar with the Corporate Social Responsibility transformation tools: SDGs, Ecosystem analysis, planetary boundaries, materiality matrix,
- Adopt a system-thinking mindset to understand the externalities of your business and your positive and negative impact on all stakeholders,
- Be true to the original intentions of marketing going back to basics,
- Take a collaborative mindset looking for winning partnerships with stakeholders,
- Demonstrate care in targeting unmet needs that serve the planet and society and developing objectives for your marketing strategy and marketing mix that address the three pillars of sustainability: People, Planet, and Profit,
- Be transparent and honest in measuring impact over the entire life cycle of your products,
- Build trust and ensure consistency between say and do as well as across the company,
- Be bold in setting ambitious yet realistic sustainability-driven objectives,
- Be a champion for transverse corporate approaches and partner with all functions in the organization to align marketing objectives and actions with the company strategy.

> ### ⊞ Takeaway
>
> Marketing now has a commendable opportunity—one that can transform our economic systems toward sustainability. We are entering a new era for marketing: the one of *Positive Impact Marketing*. Positive Impact Marketing will look to transform businesses into positive impact businesses: businesses that have a holistic positive impact on society and environment embedded at their core.

Applying the new rules of marketing

There are two major phases in the marketing strategy process. The first phase is the strategic marketing phase. In this phase, the strategy is developed. To develop the right strategy, the marketer will seek to better understand the market, customer needs, what to offer, how to position the company's offering and the company's differentiating value proposition. The next phase is the implementation phase of the strategy. In this phase, the strategy is broken down into the marketing mix and the control plan to ensure successful operationalization and implementation of the marketing strategy (Figure 2.4).

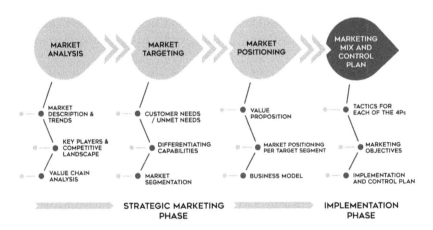

Figure 2.4 The marketing strategy process.

A strategic marketing phase enhanced with a holistic and purpose-driven approach

The traditional strategic marketing phase can be summarized in three key activities:

1 Market analysis

   • Understand the market landscape: what market we are in, how it is evolving, what are the key trends, who are the key players, what is the value chain, what is the competitive landscape and position.

2 Market targeting

   • Understand customer needs: which are the unmet needs,
   • Understand capabilities: what are the defining and differentiating capabilities for the company, how can we address unmet needs, how can we strengthen our capabilities, what adjacent or complementary capabilities should we acquire,
   • Segment the market based on needs and capabilities and define target markets.

3 Market positioning

   • Define the value proposition: what is the value proposition to targeted customers,
   • Set positioning objectives for each target market,
   • Define the business model.

Considering the opportunity for Positive Impact Marketing versus traditional marketing, we can see how these three steps of strategic marketing become not only critical but also more complex.

For market analysis:

Understanding the environment will require an additional layer of consideration, factoring in all stakeholders and the entire ecosystem not only for a given product or service but also as it relates to the entire company and the complete life cycle. This analysis will no longer be a "one-way" exercise—focused on the impact to the company—but a two-way process looking also at the external impact of the product, service, and the company: the *externalities*.

For market targeting:

When it comes to customer needs, we must ensure the market strategy is not designed to create wants but instead looks to address unmet needs as they relate to sustainability challenges. For example, as we design a new product, we will want to think about the needs of the customer as well as sustainability considerations, such as what raw material to use, how and where to source these or how to dispose of the product, and whether the customer needs to buy the product or could it be shared.

When assessing capabilities, the opportunity to create partnerships should take on a completely new dimension. The objective shall be to look for complementarity rather than pure competition. How could we collaborate with other companies so that together we can bring a new, more impactful solution? To identify these types of partners, the marketer will need to look beyond the traditional value chain or competitive landscape and will have to start from the stakeholder mapping and impact analysis.

For market positioning:

Considering the evolution of consumer needs and the opportunity to influence these, the positioning exercise will be more complex than in traditional marketing. Beyond the traditional aspects of price and performance, the marketer will have to consider a third axis with socio-ecological aspects. Positive Impact Marketing aims to influence the consumer beyond the traditional price/performance criteria. This should be part of the value proposition.

Also, when developing the marketing strategy, consistency and alignment with sustainability efforts across the company is critical. This is a guarantee against overlooking the total impact of a company, creating suspicion and ultimately greenwashing. The purpose of the brand should be fully aligned with the purpose of the company.

Considering the objectives of Positive Impact Marketing, we now see how the strategic part of marketing is key and must evolve (Figure 2.5). This will be the core of the proposed **Connect 4 Impact** methodology.

Figure 2.5 The evolution of the strategic marketing phase.

A straightforward role for the marketing mix and control plan

Let's have a look now at the implementation phase of the marketing strategy. It starts with defining the marketing mix, which is basically the operationalization of the strategy. The objective is to define the marketing strategy in a way that makes it measurable and observable. Traditional marketing is based on a marketing mix typically defined by the 4Ps—Product, Price, Place, and Promotion—with each having its own strategy or tactics.

• Product strategy: ensuring that the business's product or service is relevant to the customer's needs,
• Price strategy: setting the right price for both the customer and the business, which can be based on cost or on value created,
• Place strategy: defining the route to market, where and how the customer can buy the product or service,
• Promotion strategy: telling the target customers about the product or service.

The CIM proposes three other marketing mix Ps for businesses to think about:

• People: consider the company culture and how the staff behaves and serves the customers.
• Process: improve how the customer engages with your business.
• Physical evidence: have evidence of the product or service claims.

With the increase in green marketing, we see even more Ps included in the marketing mix, such as *partnerships* or *planet* to address societal impact.

Some sustainable marketing approaches propose a 4Cs concept that redefines the emphasis of the traditional marketing mix from:

• *Product to customer solution*: increase the emphasis toward the needs of end users and the search for solutions. Thus, we are looking at the holistic needs of a customer, including addressing potential side effects and collateral impacts. This is all the more critical as sustainable marketing aims to address the most pressing needs and not creating wants. For example, sustainable marketers look at the need for mobility and not just point-to-point transportation. That is, they look for solutions to eliminate or reduce driving and not just to replace gas engine cars with electric cars,
• *Price to (total) cost*: look at the cost of a product across its entire life cycle and propose a value pricing approach based on the total net

benefit. In an ideal economic system, the total cost would also include adjacent costs to society and environment. For example, include impact on public health into the cost of cigarettes,

- *Place to convenience*: consider all new channels to market, their respective impact, the entire purchasing process of the users, and in particular the quest for information, as well as new economic models such as the circular economy or the sharing economy. For example, make it easy for the customer to recycle the product after its use,
- *Promotion to communication*: emphasis on the need to create trust with the users, establishing a bi-directional approach through relationship building. For example, the use of certified labels will be a way to establish trust in product claims.

There are even more variations of these definitions, which begin to get extremely complex.

In fact, the complexity described above is counter-productive and has become a distraction to the original role of the marketing mix.

As acknowledged by the CIM or the 4Cs approach, the impact of the traditional 4Ps needs to support sustainability development. However, adding complexity in the marketing mix through up to 7 or 8 Ps or creating new terminologies is not the best way for considerations such as people, planet, or partnerships to be integrated in the 4Ps.

Instead, these considerations are baked into the strategic marketing phase—that is, the market analysis, market targeting, and marketing positioning activities. While strategic marketing and its three steps is a key phase in traditional marketing, it is often too quickly performed. For Positive Impact Marketing, these steps *before* defining the marketing mix become critical. This is where the broader scope and systemic approach needed to establish positive impact businesses will be analyzed and integrated in the business model. Considerations such as partnerships, people, planet, or physical evidence need to take place in this strategic marketing phase.

Thus, the marketing mix supports sustainable development because it is the outcome or operationalization of a more holistic marketing strategy. With a solid strategy developed at the start of the planning process, the marketing mix becomes more of a set of operational choices or tactics to deliver on that strategy. Likewise, the control plan shall deliver on its objectives, which is essentially to ensure that the strategy has actually been put into action in the short, middle, and longer term. It is critical, of course, that the marketing mix and control plan be fully consistent with the marketing strategy.

In sum, as long as the strategic marketing phase (marketing analysis, targeting, and positioning) is built with a systemic approach that takes

Figure 2.6 The marketing mix and control plan.

society, environment, stakeholders, and life cycle into consideration, the 4 Ps are all we need to implement a sustainable development marketing strategy (Figure 2.6).

 **Takeaway**

The opportunity for the Positive Impact Marketer is to increase focus on the strategic marketing steps (marketing analysis, targeting, and positioning) of the marketing strategy process. In doing this, the marketer will have to take a new mindset and ensure that a holistic and purposeful approach is being taken. When it comes to the implementation through the marketing mix and control plan, reaching a full alignment with that strategy and over time will be critical to avoid greenwashing.

A new methodology to complement the marketing strategy process: Connect 4 Impact

The major activities of the marketing strategy process should evolve to ensure integration of sustainability concepts. Market analysis will have to take a broader scope and include externalities for the business. Market targeting will have to consider needs related to sustainability challenges as well as look for complementarities and not rivalry with other market players. Market positioning will have to ensure a strong focus on purpose toward positive socio-ecological impact and guarantee full alignment with corporate objectives and strategy.

How can we best integrate the sustainable marketing concepts into the strategic marketing process? The answer can be found in the Sustainable Development Goals (SDGs) from the United Nations, which are certainly a key reference to what it takes to reach a sustainable development.

When looking at the 17 goals, many of them are deeply interconnected. For example, we cannot achieve SDG 11: "Make cities and human settlement inclusive, safe, resilient and sustainable" without focusing on SDG 10 "reduce inequalities" or SDG 8 "decent work and economic growth" or SDG 12 "Responsible consumption and Production" or SDG 7 "Affordable and Clean energy," and this could go on and on … In this respect, the SDG 17 "Partnerships for the goals" is probably one of the most fundamental. Forming partnerships requires systemic approaches. Systemic approaches are addressing the underlying issues for each problem. They solve these in a sustainable way, meaning in a holistic way, from the roots and for the longer term. Thus, systemic approaches are fundamental to a sustainable development.

A key word to summarize this paradigm shift to systemic thinking and approach is CONNECT. Connecting the dots has always been a key attribute of marketing—whether it comes to developing new solutions, understanding and addressing customer needs, or communicating to target audiences. Positive Impact Marketing must go a step beyond, connecting all the dots within and around the product and company. This involves going through a comprehensive and holistic analysis of all stakeholders, all needs, and all capabilities, and looking at the entire value chain over the entire life cycle of each product. This can be achieved through the strategic marketing process—one that is then fully consistent across the marketing mix and control plan.

While taking a systemic and holistic approach is key to sustainable development, it can yet seem overwhelming for the marketer or business leader. The intent here is to try to make it easier to grasp and turn to reality. Thinking through all these sustainability-related concepts, there are four key areas where this connection must happen.

The Positive Impact Marketer will thus have to make sure to:

- **Connect Stakeholders.** Connecting stakeholders begins with identifying all stakeholders, including the critical social and environmental stakeholders, then forming partnerships that lead to greater positive impact,
- **Connect Needs and Capabilities.** Positive Impact Marketers do not address needs based on wants but rather needs based on what is good for society and for the planet—including the needs of future generations. This connection can lead to systemic innovations for greater positive impact,
- **Connect Beginning and Ends.** In defining business models and developing value propositions, Positive Impact Marketers use life cycle assessments and circular economy principles to ensure the positive impact of business on society through time,
- **Connect Say and Do.** Positive Impact Marketers must ensure that environmental and social objectives join economic objectives and that stated objectives are met.

These four connections are at the heart of my methodology for Positive Impact Marketing called **Connect 4 Impact.**

The idea is not to redesign the marketing process. As explained earlier, the traditional marketing tools apply. Yet it is key to add a new mindset, captured in these four connections, that expands the boundaries of traditional marketing. These four elements will strongly impact the strategic marketing steps but will obviously need to be incorporated into the whole marketing mix and control plan. In the next four chapters, we will consider tools that will help the Positive Impact Marketer complement traditional marketing practices and implement this mindset (Figure 2.7).

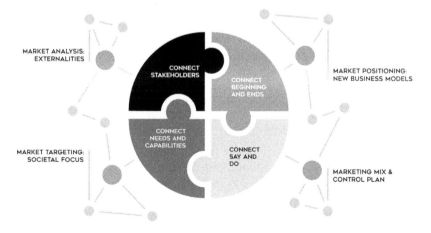

Figure 2.7 The **Connect 4 Impact** methodology.

 **Testimony**

Rethinking well-being through ecologically sustainable needs satisfiers

Sascha Nick—EPFL (Ecole Polytechnique Fédérale de Lausanne), researcher, Laboratory of Environmental and Urban Economics

At the core of my work, I use the framework of human needs and satisfiers to understand how to transform society and companies towards sustainability. People have a small set of basic human needs, such as health, including physical and mental health, protection, autonomy, affection, and/or opportunities to participate. Needs are fixed. They are universal and don't change over time or across cultures.

Satisfiers are the means through which we meet these needs. For example, a shirt is a satisfier because it satisfies the need for protection. Food is a satisfier for subsistence and health, but could also satisfy the need for participation, creation (cooking), or affection or identity.

Food is what we call a "synergistic" satisfier because it satisfies more than one need at the same time. We can eat exactly the same food, but eating that food in bad conditions or when we're alone is not nearly as nice as having a nice dinner with your friends. "Singular" satisfiers only satisfy one need, but that's fine as long as the quantity of resources needed to produce that satisfier is limited. For example, insurance can only satisfy the need for protection and that's fine. A satisfier that needs a lot of resources, for example, your house, for example, should satisfy more than just the need for protection.

While we can't change needs, we can choose the satisfiers for those needs. Over time and place and history, people have had different clothes or have eaten different things. This is how companies can transform their impact on our world: by creating satisfiers, in the form of products or services, that positively rather than negatively impact our world.

Unfortunately, we have spent the last 50 years or more producing bad satisfiers that made no sense from a societal perspective.

Processed food, fast fashion, and owning cars because in many parts of the world it's hard to do anything without a car are satisfiers with negative impacts that were intentionally created. Decades of poor planning, which created the need for cars, were very much encouraged by companies that stood to benefit, such as oil and car companies.

Creating a market for something and somehow convincing people to buy something that they don't need may help the profitability of a company, but the society that allows a company to exist and appropriate societal, scarce resources just to make a profit without really producing something useful for society is not going to survive a long time.

Tools such as the Lifecyle Analysis will help companies understand the impact of their activities. Interviewing customers can help identify if their products are or could be made to be synergistic satisfiers. For example, food can be produced in many different ways organically, as a monoculture, in some kind of agroecological environment, with or without pesticides or fertilizer. The food could come from New Zealand or from the south of Switzerland. All of these things are going to have very different impacts on sustainability—impacts you identify from lifecycle analysis.

I'm working on several projects related to needs and satisfiers. Perhaps the most important one is a project that looks into transforming the Swiss built environment. So that's buildings, mobility between buildings, open spaces—pretty much everything that is built up, but which can be transformed in a way that will allow us to live well with a lot fewer resources.

For housing, for example, the issues on the environmental side are linked to the quantity of resources, such as resources needed to heat them. But we also need to rethink our dominant mental model of a house as a building for a single family with cars. If we get beyond this mental model—and this is what we are studying—we can change things very significantly. For example, which buildings do we keep or not keep? How do we renovate them to get them to the right level of energy efficiency without using too many materials?

Bottom line, we can't change needs, but we can very well choose the satisfier. And if we want to live sustainably, we need to organize society in a way that our needs are satisfied through ecologically sustainable synergistic satisfiers.

Bibliography

Frank-Martin Belz and Ken Peattie *Sustainability marketing—A global perspective.* Wiley edition, 2012.

Chapter 3

Connect Stakeholders

MARKET ANALYSIS: EXTERNALITIES

CONNECT STAKEHOLDERS

- ☑ ECOSYSTEM ANALYSIS
- ☑ STAKEHOLDER MAPPING
- ☑ FORMING IMPACTFUL PARTNERSHIPS

Figure 3.1 Connect Stakeholders.

The first element of the **Connect 4 Impact** methodology, Connect Stakeholders, aligns with the first step of traditional strategic marketing: market analysis. Key activities for this element include; ecosystem analysis, stakeholder mapping and forming impactful partnerships (Figure 3.1)

As explained earlier, considering the sustainability challenges ahead, we need system thinking and a systemic approach enabled by Positive Impact Marketing. The scope of the connections in the strategic planning process is one of the fundamental differences between a traditional and a sustainable business approach. There are two different components that make this scope broader: one is related to the externalities, direct and indirect, and the other one to the time scale. Traditional marketers conduct a *market* analysis. Positive Impact Marketers conduct an *ecosystem* analysis.

What is meant here by "ecosystem," which is sometimes referred to as "business ecosystem"? As explained in Chapter 1, each of the entities in an ecosystem impacts and is impacted by the other entities, resulting in a completely interrelated relationship within and across the entities and over time. Thus, all of the entities in an ecosystem are connected to each other.

To identify and create these connections, it is important to first *complete a holistic ecosystem analysis*. During the ecosystem analysis, the Positive Impact Marketer can identify both the direct and indirect impacts of the company's offering on the company's environment over time.

DOI: 10.4324/9781003422709-4

After completing an ecosystem analysis, the next step in the Connect Stakeholders phase of the **Connect 4 Impact** methodology is to finalize the identification of all stakeholders through *stakeholder mapping*. Mapping stakeholders serves two major benefits for the Positive Impact Marketer:

- Further assesses externalities of the business including all environmental as well as social impacts. Complementing the consideration of the planetary boundaries, it includes the impact on all stakeholders, including the local community or employees, and considers the impact on stakeholders throughout the entire life cycle of the company offering,
- Identifies possible partnerships to develop high-impact solutions to targeted unmet needs. As explained earlier, transformative change requires holistic approaches.

The final step of this phase is to *establish impactful partnerships* that will strengthen the company's long-term positive social and environmental impact.

Ecosystem analysis

As with traditional marketing, the priority of the Positive Impact Marketer is to understand the environment of the business. However, the scope of what is analyzed in this step of the strategic marketing phase will differ. While traditional marketing looks primarily at the direct environment of the business, positive impact businesses go beyond and thoroughly assess both direct and indirect impacts. Factoring in company externalities and planetary boundaries is necessary in developing sustainable solutions and business models.

Therefore, ecosystem analysis is a critical first step toward Positive Impact Marketing. Before analyzing the externalities and planetary boundaries, however, it is important to first consider the megatrends related to the company and analyze the environment in which the business is evolving through the lens of sustainability challenges. This megatrends analysis is also a key way to ensure that the ecosystem is considered not only for today's stakeholders but for future generations.

Megatrends analysis

Megatrends can be identified in several ways and are influenced by the sector in which the company operates. We usually find megatrends falling under the categories of technology, ecology, and socio-economic (Figure 3.2).

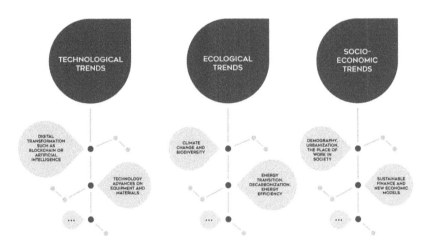

Figure 3.2 Megatrends analysis.

The technological trends are probably those that have been given constant consideration by marketers. What are the technologies that are already in place today or expected to transform the landscape of the company and product? Technology advances can happen in many aspects of a business in particular, materials, equipment, or processes.

Ecological trends are more and more significant for companies. They relate to climate change, biodiversity impacts, decarbonation, or energy efficiency needs. These are critical for the Positive Impact Marketer to consider in the ecosystem analysis.

Likewise, socio-economic trends must be a strong consideration for the Positive Impact Marketer. They include trends that affect society such as urbanization, demography, or new economic models to enable sustainability.

Understanding the megatrends evolving in an industry and market of a company is critical in strategic marketing. This is typically done in traditional marketing although it often remains a somewhat remote input to the marketing strategy and is often primarily focused on technological trends. When it comes to Positive Impact Marketing, identifying mega-trends related to sustainability—including ecological trends and socio-economic trends must take place at this initial step. Sustainability-related trends help assess the social and environmental impact of this business today *and tomorrow*. As explained earlier, sustainability marketing requires a broader scope in space—through indirect impacts—and in time, through the full life cycle of products and to serve the needs of future generations.

Assessing externalities

There are several tools and frameworks available to traditional marketing that can be applied to analyze the environment of a company or business.

A well-known way to analyze is using Porter's Five Forces Framework created by Harvard Business School professor Michael E. Porter in 1979. These forces include:

- The number and power of a company's competitive rivals,
- The threat of new entrants and barriers to entry,
- The bargaining power of suppliers and customers based on their number, uniqueness, or ability, and cost to substitute,
- The threat of substitutes based on substitute performance and cost of change.

As we can see, this tool is primarily focused on identifying forces that have an impact on profitability. It is also very focused on direct impacts to a given company or product.

Another framework often used in traditional marketing to understand the environment for a given product or service is the SWOT (strengths, weaknesses, opportunities, and threats) analysis. A SWOT analysis assesses internal and external factors, as well as current and future potential. It is therefore a tool for not only analyzing the environment but also defining the opportunity and the value proposition. Here again, this tool is very focused on profitability and direct impacts.

While these tools help the marketer examine the environment of the company from both internal and external sources, they are insufficient to make a thorough analysis of all the impacts of the company in its world. Understanding the impact of the activities of the business on the environment and on all relevant stakeholders must take place to establish a sustainable business model. This includes examining the aspects related to externalities, meaning both direct and indirect impacts. As explained previously, understanding the externalities of a business is key to sustainable development. This analysis will be a basis for developing a value proposition and business model that contributes to sustainable development. We'll come back in a following chapter.

The tools available for corporate social responsibility strategy development are excellent tools to assess the externalities of a business. The materiality assessment and matrix is one of the most commonly used methodologies to develop sustainability reports and strategies.

A materiality analysis and materiality matrix help companies prioritize sustainability issues to focus on. The materiality matrix uses contrasting two dimensions: the importance of the issue to the company and the importance of the issue to stakeholders. Materiality matrices can be found in sustainability reports published by public companies. This tool is also detailed in the ISO 26000 norm.

The materiality matrix is hence a great tool for the Positive Impact Marketer to gain a holistic understanding of the environment of the product and company as well as their impact, direct and indirect, on all stakeholders. This analysis should complement the traditional environment analysis.

The SDGs and tools made available by the United Nations—in particular, the SDG Action Manager tool developed by the UN Global Compact and B lab—are also very relevant in assessing the externalities of a business. The SDG Action Manager is a web-based impact management tool designed to help businesses set goals in alignment with the SDGs and assess how the business is performing against each of the SDGs. This evaluation helps identify the externalities of a company and product and thus complete the full ecosystem analysis. From this, you can then select which SDGs are most relevant to your business or what to prioritize.

There are other tools available for this type of analysis, but most are more focused on specific aspects.

Although not specifically designed to support businesses in assessment of externalities, the planetary boundaries framework is particularly useful in gaining a holistic perspective of the externalities of a business on the earth system. The planetary boundaries framework was developed in 2009 by scientists from the Stockholm Resilience Center. The planetary boundaries refer to the limits of six categories of human activities beyond which the ability of future generations to survive and thrive is threatened by large-scale environmental changes. The latest planet boundaries report, which dates from 2023, states that these boundaries have been breached in six areas: biosphere integrity, climate change, introduction of novel entities in the environment, biogeochemical flows, land-system change, and freshwater use.

Since it was developed, this planetary boundaries framework has generated enormous interest within science, policy, and practice circles. This framework is highly recommended as a reference and tool for businesses to assess their externalities to the environment. In order to better assess these externalities, it will be critical for the Positive Impact Marketer to establish a close collaboration with environmental experts within or outside the company.

Takeaway

The first step of traditional strategic marketing—market analysis—must be much more holistic and systemic in Positive Impact Marketing. We shall hence refer to this step as ecosystem analysis. This step focuses on sustainability-related environmental and socio-economic megatrends in addition to familiar technological trends, and externalities of the company and product or service. Using tools and concepts from corporate social responsibility such as the materiality matrix, SDG action manager, or planetary boundaries framework along with traditional market environment analysis tools ensures that the necessary focus on externalities and long-term impacts are taken into consideration.

Stakeholder mapping

As explained previously, sustainability requires a transformation from a shareholder economy to a stakeholder economy. This means a shift from focusing on shareholders and short-term profit to focusing on stakeholders and long-term social and environmental impact. It is hence critical for the Positive Impact Marketer to identify all stakeholders through thorough stakeholder mapping (Figure 3.3).

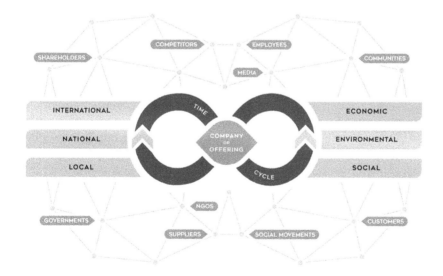

Figure 3.3 Stakeholder mapping.

Stakeholders in the value chain

The most obvious stakeholders of a company can be found along the value chain.

The concept of a value chain as a decision support tool was added to the competitive strategies paradigm developed by Michael E. Porter in 1979. Porter's Value Chain concept established the basic understanding of value chains generally accepted today. The key activities within the value chain as defined by Porter include inbound logistics, operations, outbound logistics, marketing and sales, and service. This is where competitors will also usually be captured. These are categorized as primary activities. Secondary activities include procurement, human resource management, technological development, and infrastructure. The value chain is thus a rudimentary mapping of the stakeholders present in the progression of the product or service from raw materials to the end user.

Yet this value chain approach is very focused on the company's own operations and needs. For a value chain analysis to effectively support sustainability, it must incorporate a broader view of each link in the chain. The result will be a new set of social, environmental, and economic stakeholders. In the automobile industry, for example, we would expand the analysis beyond the components, but to each element of the component. We would, for example, include in the value chain the materials used to formulate the coating for the body of a car. We would then identify new stakeholders—in this case, the providers of the ingredients for that coating formulation. This focus on the upstream end of the value chain is becoming more and more integrated in traditional marketing. The analysis of the value chain should also be expanded in another way, specifically beyond the supposed "end" of the value chain. Unfortunately, today most of these value chain analyses are performed in a linear fashion. This means that the product flow is seen with a beginning and an end where the end is waste. An expanded analysis of a value chain would identify how this waste can be a resource for another value chain, thus, creating a more circular process.

In the meantime, if the value chain analysis is constrained to its traditional parameters and focused on short-term profit, it can only represent a part of the stakeholders. An expanded value chain analysis helps identify a new set of stakeholders.

Social and environmental stakeholders along the entire life cycle

To prepare a more thorough stakeholder mapping, the marketer must consider social and environmental externalities. Mapping to this extent goes beyond traditional value chain mapping and is critical to make the necessary connections for Positive Impact Marketing.

In the *social* category of stakeholders, we find groups such as local communities and inhabitants, employees, government bodies shaping policies, pressure groups, and media. These stakeholders in the social realm must be considered in creating a sustainable business model. First, because the social aspects are key to the sustainability development goals. A business model that relies on child labor or ignores the impact on local communities cannot be a sustainable business model. Similarly, a business model that doesn't respect diversity and inclusion in the workforce cannot lead to sustainable solutions simply because they may not be representative of the user base. Second, considering the paradigm change involved, sustainability transformation will not happen without the involvement and ownership of the people who are inhabitants, end users, and citizens. Thus, it is critical to integrate these in the stakeholder mapping and business model. The energy sector provides a good illustration of this. For the energy transition to happen, it is key for businesses to cooperate with governments as well as make the inhabitants part of the solution. This is the case for energy efficiency solutions as well as self-production with houses' solar systems for example.

Stakeholders that fall into the *environmental* category are first of all the planet, fauna, and flora, as well as biodiversity. The Positive Impact Marker must have those as primary stakeholders. Those stakeholders are typically represented by nongovernmental (NGOs) or nonprofit organizations (NPOs).

Under the environmental category, one will also find stakeholders linked to the business activities and with environmental impacts and in particular greenhouse gas (GHG) emissions. Here again, tools from corporate social responsibility will be useful for the Positive Impact Marketer to identify environmental stakeholders.

Scope 1, 2, and 3 emissions are the global standard framework, launched in 1998 under the GHG Protocol, for classifying and measuring greenhouse gas emissions. This framework is used to develop corporate social responsibility strategies by guiding the company to consider three types of emissions:

- Scope 1 are direct emissions from the operations of a company,
- Scope 2 are the indirect emissions of a company, those created by resources purchased to enable operations, such as energy,
- Scope 3 are indirect value chain emissions created along the supply chain upstream and downstream.

Scopes 1 and 2 are emissions owned or controlled by a company whereas scope 3 emissions are result of activities of the company but not owned or controlled by it.

By looking at these three types of emissions, the Positive Impact Marketer will be able to identify a new set of stakeholders, such as energy suppliers (Scope 2) or the manufacturer of components for the company's product (Scope 3). The scope 3 emissions will be key to identify stakeholders along the entire life cycle of a product or service.

Integrating stakeholders impacting scope 1, 2 and 3 emissions in the ecosystem analysis will be critical to develop a very holistic stakeholder map and thus design more sustainable solutions and business models. Here again, we see how the toolkit of corporate social responsibility can be useful to the Positive Impact Marketer.

Multiple geographic scales

Another consideration when looking to identify stakeholders is linked to the multiple levels of impact from a geographical standpoint: local, national, and international. Who could be impacted by a local business on a broader scale? Let's take the "butterfly effect" where a small action can have major impact elsewhere. A similar concept can apply here—the impact on a given local biodiversity can have repercussions for a different part of the world. We are experiencing more and more of this effect, or perhaps it is becoming more and more visible. This increasing visibility is particularly evident the other way around—that is, when the global activities of an international business have local impacts on biodiversity or local communities. When looking at the different geographic scales, we can identify possible local economic or social partners, which can alleviate that possible negative impact. This practice is more and more common with businesses using local agriculture such as coffee or tea.

With geographic scale also comes the ability to identify best practices or solutions available in other areas of the world. By doing so, we can rapidly identify a new set of stakeholders and potential partners. This implies taking a different mindset, one of collaboration versus competition. The Positive Impact Marketer will thus look for complementarities rather than direct competition. Sharing these best practices across geographies is a key value brought by some NPOs.

 Definition

Stakeholder mapping: This is the process of uncovering and identifying all of the possible stakeholders that could be impacted directly or indirectly by the activities of a company. For the stakeholder mapping to be holistic and thorough, it is key to consider internal and external stakeholders, direct and indirect impacts, social and environmental aspects, as well as multiple scales in time and geography.

Takeaway

By performing holistic stakeholder mapping, the Positive Impact Marketer can get to a thorough assessment of all externalities, thus mitigating negative impacts and increasing positive impacts of the business. The traditional value chain analysis tool should be completed with thorough stakeholder mapping considering direct and indirect impacts, social and environmental aspects at multiple geographic scales as well as the entire life cycle of the company's offering.

Forming impactful partnerships

The ecosystem analysis completed with thorough stakeholder mapping enables the Positive Impact Marketer to assess the externalities of the product, service, and company, which is fundamental to establish positive impact businesses.

Such analysis serves two major benefits that contribute to an even greater virtuous circle and thus positive impact:

• Identification of sustainability challenges and hence business opportunities,
• Identification of potential partners toward greater positive impact.

To increase the positive impact of a business, however, requires not only identifying stakeholders but also connecting them to each other. Thus, the final step in the Connect Stakeholders phase of **Connect 4 Impact** is to form impactful partnerships.

Once the stakeholder mapping is achieved, the key is to define how to Connect Stakeholders. That connection must be strong and impactful meaning leading to a greater positive impact. It is essential to form partnerships that will sustain positive impact in the short, mid, and long term. To do this, the stakeholder mapping will have to include the respective needs of the stakeholders based on who they are and their mission.

Thus, it is key to identify the nature and flow of impacts among them.

For each stakeholder, it will be important to first understand their respective mission, objectives, and needs. Then the interrelation between stakeholders must be clarified. In other words, why is this stakeholder a stakeholder? And to what extent? For example, in the case of a local business, to what extent will the business be impacted, and what are the respective competitive situations, value propositions, and business models? This will also have to be done by integrating a time scale. When is the stakeholder a stakeholder? Does that evolve over time?

Understanding these interrelations will enable us to look for winning partnerships through complementarities.

NGOs and NPOs are good sources for facilitating connections on essential needs with the focus on externalities and sustainability. Take, for example, the NPO of Alliance to End Plastic Waste (AEPW). AEPW is made up of 50 major plastics companies forming the largest public-private partnership ever created and is focused on solutions that will minimize and manage plastic waste and promote post-use solutions. By forming such partnerships with a commendable mission, these companies should be in a better position to solve challenges linked to the plastic industry.

The World Business Council for Sustainable Development (WBCSD) is an NPO that brings together connected stakeholders to collaborate on sustainability initiatives. For example, its OP2B (One Planet Business for Biodiversity) initiative brings together a coalition of stakeholders in or related to the agricultural sector. The goal is to protect and restore biodiversity through the action of the stakeholders, participation of institutional and financial decision-makers, and policy recommendations. The initiative's mission is to increase regenerative agriculture and culti-vated biodiversity and protect ecosystems.

These organizations thus offer great platforms to form partnerships among stakeholders looking for commonalities in their respective missions.

Positive impact businesses will look to integrate these partnerships in their business model. It is only when partnerships are part of the business model that they can lead to greater positive impact.

For collaborations to be impactful, there are five key principles to follow beyond targeting positive impact:

- **Win-win:** Each partnership that forms these collaborations must be based on a win-win formula where each partner gets a positive outcome that matters to its core objective and aligns to its vision and mission. This seems obvious but is fundamental and is unfortunately not always in place. In traditional business models, marketers and business leaders were primarily focused on extracting profit for their organization not giving equal focus to benefits to major stakeholders,
- **Objectives:** The objectives of the partnership must be clear and ambitious yet realistic, with progress that can be measured on the way,

- **Commitment:** Each partner must be committed and reliable with regard to the stated objectives. This requires consistency and long-term commitment,
- **Transparency:** Clarity and transparency must be guaranteed to strengthen the trust between partners. What each part brings to the table and gets out of it must be clear, balanced, and equitable,
- **Mindset:** A collaborative, inclusive, and respectful or caring mindset is a prerequisite. Looking for complementarities and how we can be stronger together is an essential part of that required mindset. There's a famous African proverb that summarizes it all: "Alone we go faster. Together we go further." Thus, cultural aspects are central to such partnerships.

Such partnerships will be called impactful partnerships. These are partnerships that once integrated in the business model will guarantee a sustainable positive impact.

 Takeaway

Collaborations are key to positive impact and sustainable business models. They are formed with stakeholders beyond the value chain and within the entire ecosystem. For these collaborations to become impactful partnerships, they must abide by a few fundamental principles: win-win formulas; clear, ambitious yet realistic objectives that can be measured; commitment and transparency from partners; and last but not least a new underlying collaborative and caring mindset.

 Testimony

Managers should be obsessed with satisfying their stakeholders

Christian Brunier—CEO Industrial Services Geneva (SIG)
Satisfying their stakeholders, from owners to employees, from customers to societal movements, is the holy grail for companies claiming to be good corporate citizens. Managers must be obsessed with the common good. The value created for stakeholders must be not only economic, but also ecological and social. It must aim for balance and sustainability. The profit-at-all-costs approach, with no consideration for stakeholders, has driven us into a wall.

As an energy company, SIG advocates "less and better consumption" to meet the challenges of the climate emergency. As a public service company, SIG seeks cooperation with the local economic fabric (SMEs, SMIs, start-ups) to multiply its actions. Together, we are always stronger. For example, SIG has developed an intelligent lighting concept for building communal areas. Geneva's electrical companies are now installing them. Smaller in size, they operate at lower cost and can be installed more quickly.

The same synergistic relationship exists with heating engineers. SIG builds renewable thermal highways (ecological heating and cooling), large networks, and major works. Small networks and boiler rooms are the preserve of local private companies. By working together and making the most of each other's skills and strengths, we can achieve Geneva's energy transition objectives more quickly.

This logic guides all aspects of our energy-saving program, known as "Eco21." It may seem paradoxical for an energy distributor to encourage its customers to consume less. Yet, this is the role of a responsible company, and all the more so for a public sector one. Hospitals, whether public or private, don't encourage patients to drink and smoke in order to get more patients. Reducing consumption is part of the same public good logic for an energy company. Having customers consuming less also proves positive in terms of our business model by reducing our purchase of energy—since we produce locally only a third of the electricity consumed by our customers in the Canton of Geneva—and therefore our energy dependence. Relying less on imported energy further strengthens our business model because all electricity produced locally is from renewable sources and supports the local economy. Less consumption has the added benefit of cutting peak consumption, which is very costly on the market. Our customers also want to optimize their bills. Our competitors cut prices for a short period; we cut consumption, which is more sustainable. In this way, we build customer loyalty, creating a sort of "consume well" community by improving both our customers' ecological footprint and their bills.

This program has created numerous jobs at SIG and elsewhere. For an energy-saving program to be successful, it's important to stimulate the ecosystem. We have therefore contributed to the training in energy efficiency of electricians, heating engineers, engineers, and architects. It's the combination of the power of public service and the agility of small and medium-sized businesses that contributes to stakeholder satisfaction in these areas. Eco21 promotes all aspects of sustainable development: ecological, economic, and social.

In the same spirit of synergy with our stakeholders, our staff is very much involved, contributing through informal and formal meetings ideas and solutions for reaching our goal. Our stakeholders are also represented on our Board of Directors.

Successful stakeholder management requires a love of people, a concern for the collective good, and, above all, an ability to multiply interactions. By listening to and dialoguing with all our stakeholders, we give priority to relationships, often informal, and to cohesion. In the spirit of this informality as we work together to find solutions, negotiations at key stages in our history have always taken place behind the scenes, never in formal meetings.

Eco21, a collective success

By 2022, the eco21 program will have saved 252 GWh/year of electricity since its inception in 2007, or 8.5% of Geneva's total consumption. And this even though the population has grown by 25% over the same period. In Geneva, electricity consumption per inhabitant in 2021 is equivalent to the consumption level of 1985. This reflects a reduction of 509,000 tons of CO_2 since 2007 (-0.8% per year) and an electricity bill for the people of Geneva reduced by 43 million Swiss Francs (CHF).

The eco21 program sets all players in motion with more than 200 partner heating specialists, electricians, ventilation engineers, sanitary engineers, solar engineers, and engineering firms working to achieve the energy transition. The program thus creates wealth and jobs. SIG trains 500 to 700 professionals every year. Eco21 has invested 164 million francs in Geneva since its inception, generating 572 million CHF of investment in the local economy. In addition, 780 new local jobs have been created since 2007.

Key steps

Three steps *to* Connect Stakeholders

STEP 1: Ecosystem analysis

- Identify all economic, social, and environmental megatrends that are affecting the industry or sector you operate in today and tomorrow,
- Perform an environment analysis using traditional marketing tools, the Porter forces and SWOT analysis in particular,
- Complement this analysis by assessing externalities, using corporate social responsibility tools and concepts such as the materiality matrix from ISO 26000, the SDGs action manager tool, or the planetary boundaries framework,
- Summarize a first-pass assessment of stakeholders from this ecosystem analysis.

STEP 2: Stakeholder mapping

- Position your business in its value chain, including the company value chain and industry value chain,
- Identify social and environmental stakeholders, including community, government, public or local entities, pressure groups, or NGOs,
- Understand all scope 1, 2, and 3 impacts of your business to complement the environmental stakeholder analysis,
- Consider the multiple geographical scales at play and related stakeholders.

STEP 3: Forming impactful partnerships

- Understand the interrelations between stakeholders on the stakeholder map, focusing on respective needs and missions,
- Identify possible partnerships that will contribute to strengthening your positive impact,
- Validate how and if preconditions for forming impactful partnerships are met.

Chapter 4

Connect Needs and Capabilities

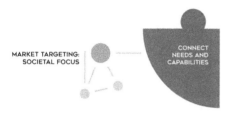

MARKET TARGETING: SOCIETAL FOCUS

CONNECT NEEDS AND CAPABILITIES

☑ PRIORITIZE CONSUMER NEEDS

☑ MATCH NEEDS AND CAPABILITIES

☑ LEVERAGE COLLECTIVE INTELLIGENCE

Figure 4.1 Connect Needs and Capabilities.

One of the major objectives of marketing is to propose solutions that create value. For this the marketer needs to first identify needs and then shape an offer to address these. When it comes to Positive Impact Marketing, it will be key to focus on the most pressing needs for society and the planet. With regard to the offer, the approach will require a systemic view of the situation and opportunity at stake (Figure 4.1).

Prioritize consumer needs

From "wants" to "most pressing needs"

Understanding unmet needs is critical for any marketing strategy. Yet the mission of Positive Impact Marketing is to meet *needs* but not to create *wants* or *desires* or encourage additional so-called customer needs without consideration of the externalities—in particular negative social and environmental impacts—of the business involved.

Remember the definition of sustainable development from the Brundtland Report (1987): "development that meets the needs of the present without compromising the ability of future generations to meet their own needs."

As sustainability marketing is all about meeting the needs and not creating wants, the challenge is to assess the most pressing unmet needs not based on wants, desire, and how to favor consumerism but rather on

DOI: 10.4324/9781003422709-5

sustainability challenges. This means analyzing consumer needs from either an environmental perspective or social or both. The Positive Impact Marketer will make sure to rethink a consumer need in terms of its impact on society and the planet and prioritize the most pressing needs.

For this reason, the ecosystem analysis and stakeholder mapping exercises described earlier are the perfect starting point for identifying and prioritizing unmet needs that, when met, will have the most positive impacts.

The megatrends analysis, an important tool for the ecosystem analysis, provides an unlimited source for unmet needs. When analyzing ecological or socio-economic trends, one can easily identify unmet needs related to sustainability. Some talk about the business opportunity of sustainability. As a marketer, it is clear that every problem is an opportunity, and actually a business opportunity. When it comes to sustainability, the challenges are so huge and so is the corresponding opportunity. As mentioned in Chapter 1, this business opportunity has been assessed to be over \$12 trillion.

SDGs help take the problem at its roots from a sustainability standpoint and thus look for those unmet needs that impact our generation and the ones to come. When looking at unmet needs for a specific food product, for example, considering different SDGs can be a good source for this positive impact assessment. The positive impact food product marketer can ask; how am I addressing SDG 2 (zero hunger) or SDG 3 (good health and well-being) or SDG6 (clean water and sanitation) or SDG 12 (responsible consumption and production) and so on. The idea is to look at the root cause for these goals and determine if the business solution can help address one or a few of these simultaneously. The UN website on SDGs provides very useful information and starting point to understand the scope and roots of these challenges.

The more we broaden the scope of ecosystem analysis, the more opportunities to fulfill social and environmentally friendly unmet needs come up. It seems obvious that if you look just at a product in isolation, the number of opportunities you will be able to identify will be narrower than if you look at the full life cycle of the product or the broader ecosystem.

For example, at the end of that life cycle, a spent product could be a resource for another business versus being only waste. Managing the waste thus represents an additional unmet need as well as an opportunity to become a resource. Integrating this in your market targeting creates de facto more opportunities to create value for the business as well as for the planet.

Likewise, understanding the externalities of your product or business and their impact on identified stakeholders helps identify ways to mitigate negative impacts or target net positive impacts. We can find an illustration of this in the field of energy. While the need for heating is essential, the choice of solutions, which can go from the heater itself to the design of the building, can make a huge difference in terms of externalities. The first priority when it comes to heating solutions should be directed to energy efficiency or building isolation solutions. This approach toward unmet needs opens up new perspectives and opportunities. Regenerative business opportunities, where one will rethink which raw material to use and how to use them, are another example of how considering externalities uncovers unmet needs that become business opportunities.

Finally, the ecosystem analysis and stakeholder mapping enable a more systemic analysis of needs. One should soon realize that when it comes to sustainability, unmet needs are interrelated just as SDGs are. For example, SDG 14 (life below water) and SDG 15 (Life on Land) are very connected to SDG 13 (climate action) or SDG 11 (Sustainable cities and communities) or SDG 7 (affordable and clean energy). Thus, one can develop strong value propositions addressing multiple needs.

As a company aims to improve its positive impact, the ecosystem analysis and stakeholder mapping will hence provide tools for Positive Impact Marketers to identify the most pressing needs. They will not only manage their business's impact on society and the environment but also identify new opportunities. Furthermore, by assessing the importance of the impact, this analysis becomes the base as well for prioritizing these opportunities toward greater impact. This brings about two types of opportunities: those mitigating negative impact and those creating net positive impact. Prioritization should be done not only based on profit but also on the net impact on society and environment thus further strengthening the total positive impact.

Responsible consumption

The Positive Impact Marketer needs to target unmet needs with positive impact, but he also has the potential to enable, influence, and drive responsible consumption.

Due to easier and instant access to information, greater awareness of sustainable living, and pressure from different organizations, consumption has become for consumers more of a process than an act. It involves more steps including information search, comparison and evaluation of alternatives, and consideration of the product impact and its post-use destiny. This consumption process represents an opportunity for the Positive Impact Marketer to influence responsible consumption through the marketing mix.

Marketing tactics in the marketing mix will guide how and where the consumer purchases, how he is handling the end of life of the product, how he contributes to greater impact through labels and certifications, etc.

All marketers involved in B2C and B2B to some degree know the traditional influencers on consumption that are typically used as levers for marketers. These include cultural needs, social needs, and personal, psychological, and situational influencers. Today, with the increasing awareness on sustainability challenges and climate change, we see that psychological influencers are becoming more and more important. Psychological influencers relate to attitudes and beliefs: what do I think is important? What does it mean for me? How do I see myself?

There is a notion of either guilt or conviction that has been exacerbated by global events whether they are weather-related (i.e., record heat and cold temperatures) or health (i.e., COVID-19 pandemic) or globalization and resource management-related (COVID-19 pandemic, Russia/Ukraine war). This is something the marketer looking to influence consumer needs toward more responsible consumption should count on.

Psychological influencers are key additional influencers for the Positive Impact Marketer. They should be leveraged to drive responsible consumption.

Thus, the Positive Impact Marketer has a mission to drive responsible consumption. To do that, it will be key that when targeting unmet needs to be addressed, the Positive Impact Marketer defines the brand purpose. The brand purpose reflects this responsible consumption mission—that is, consumer consumption that supports rather than undermines sustainability. The most famous example of brand purpose is Patagonia, which is known for its focus on activism and responsible consumption and which directs a significant part of its profits to climate change. Patagonia promotes responsible consumption by creating products that are, according to its statement of values, "useful, versatile, long-lasting, repairable, and recyclable." Another example is with Unilever and its Sustainable Living Plan launched in 2010. Through its brands, Unilever aims at addressing social inequality and climate crisis.

The brand purpose will be related to the problem it aims at solving whether it brings a social or environmental benefit or both. Finally, the brand purpose should be consistent with the company purpose as well as across the marketing mix of each product line. This is critical to establish trust with a brand or business.

 Takeaway

When identifying and prioritizing unmet needs to be addressed in the market targeting step of strategic marketing, the Positive Impact Marketer will make sure to first address pressing needs for society and the planet, rather than wants driven by consumerism. Secondly, the Positive Impact Marketer will look to define a brand purpose that helps drive responsible consumption.

Match unmet needs and capabilities

Once the most pressing unmet needs to target are identified, the next step is to match these with existing or new capabilities. Sustainability challenges at hand are so big and pressing that any new solution that helps companies and organizations to move in the right direction is key. In that sense, all solutions or innovations count!

Assessing capabilities

For a company to achieve its mission and make a profit—which will further support its mission—it must be clear about its capabilities. Specifically, what are its unique capabilities that position it to offer unique contributions to the solution needed? A company must be clear about its differentiating capabilities as well as those of its stakeholders.

Hence, the first consideration here will be to gain a thorough understanding of existing capabilities. This means capabilities already available within the company as well as outside the company.

However, as we look to develop sustainable business models and address the many challenges at hand, it is key to look for complementarities instead of increasing competition. The adage "stronger together" is particularly relevant in the face of sustainability challenges. As the world and its sustainability challenges become more complex, matching capabilities to address the most pressing unmet needs may require the formation of partnerships and the joining of capabilities. The goal is to find partners with complementary capabilities. Forming partnerships can thus be a great way to amplify capabilities.

The traditional marketer is still too often focused on getting a thorough understanding of the capabilities of its competitors and seeing how and to what extent his capabilities are unique and differentiated. The Positive Impact Marketer should go to the next level starting from the ecosystem analysis and the stakeholder mapping. He should look at the stakeholder mapping identifying capabilities not only of direct competitors but of all stakeholders. In doing this he will strive to identify complementarities. How the company's capabilities when combined with those of its stakeholders can be reinforced to address a given need?

These are the questions that the Positive Impact Marketer will want to address. This will mean mapping the company's capabilities as well as the capabilities of potential partners in and around the value chain and how they complement each other. The ecosystem analysis and stakeholder mapping performed earlier will be instrumental to achieve that step.

Innovation: Solutions for unmet needs

Innovation happens when a company or an individual brings a solution to a specific unmet need. The capabilities of that company or individual will then address that unmet need. As we think about innovation, we tend to think about the greatest game-changing innovations. Names such as Pierre & Marie Curie or Steve Jobs or Bill Gates come to mind. Thus, innovation becomes a term that may be frightening. Yet there are different levels of innovation and quick wins are probably as important as game-changing innovation when it comes to sustainability and considering the call to action.

A way to think about the different types of innovation is to look at how new a solution is in terms of either technology or use, meaning application or market. In other words, an innovation or solution is a function of a technology—existing or new—for a given application—existing or new. In the case of existing technologies for existing applications, there are still opportunities for innovation in the sense of incremental innovations leveraging existing technologies (Figure 4.2).

The easiest and quickest path to innovation is typically to start with existing technologies. How can we adjust these technologies in an existing market to deliver what we call *incremental innovation*?

There are indeed already several solutions that exist to address sustainability challenges. Seeing the urgency for action, it is critical for marketers to gain a good understanding of these existing solutions or capabilities that could address unmet needs. Take the example of energy. There are many solutions available already, from renewable energy to energy-saving solutions. In that space, it is clearly a question of how to deploy these rapidly and consistently in each territory. Despite huge improvements in the last few years, these technologies are not always competitive. Yet, it is only by scaling them up and, when needed, adjusting

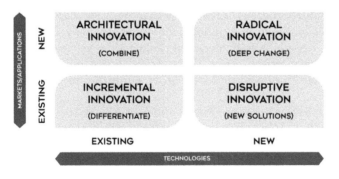

Figure 4.2 Different types of innovation.

them to the existing applications that we will achieve economies of scale that will make these competitive. It is hence critical that before investing time and effort in new technologies, marketers look at using and optimizing existing technologies for existing applications.

In other cases, existing technology could be used in new markets or to solve different challenges. These innovations are called *architectural innovations*. These are also rather quick to deploy and hence a great way to accelerate positive impact. An example of this in the Smart Cities would be how sensors using the rather mature technology of LoRa WAN—a long-range wireless communication technology that combines low power consumption and long-range can be used in many new applications. For example, these sensors can help better manage public lighting during the night, which itself has a positive impact on energy consumption as well as biodiversity or even health management.

When no existing capabilities can be used or leveraged for a given unmet need, it will then be key to invest in new technologies. Here again, there are two types of innovations with new technologies. When the application is existing, we call these *disruptive innovations*, while we refer to *radical innovations* when both the technology and the application are new.

When it comes to developing new technologies, the traditional marketer will typically collaborate either with the research department internally or look for collaborations with value chain partners—customers and suppliers in particular—and to some extent with universities. He will rarely go beyond these direct stakeholders.

In my career, I have experienced situations when sharing needs and capabilities across a value chain has helped to identify how existing capabilities of a given value chain partner could be used rather easily to solve unmet needs of other players on that value chain. This has been a deciding factor in value chains that are typically long and cross-geographies. Take the textile industry, where the connections from raw materials suppliers to the many textile players in Ethiopia or Bangladesh down to the fashion players of the Western world are complex and remote. Those players from one end to the other are sometimes disconnected so that unmet needs and hence solutions are not easy to develop and implement. For example, most often the garment producer will put forward needs such as cost reduction while the players down the value chain are driven to achieve a sustainable value proposition. By reconciling these needs, the raw material suppliers can propose solutions that address both the garment producer's cost needs and the fashion players' sustainability needs, thus making the value proposition stronger for all. An example of this would be solutions brought by the raw material suppliers for the dyeing process that help reduce energy and water usage, which has an impact on cost as well as sustainability profile.

The Positive Impact Marketer will bring this approach to the next level. He will here again start with the ecosystem analysis and stakeholder mapping to look for partnerships beyond the value chain or direct stakeholders. As explained earlier, a better understanding of needs and capabilities across the entire ecosystem helps to rapidly develop new solutions and accelerate impact.

For such innovations, partnerships with other businesses, local partners, universities, or startups can be a great accelerator if not a prerequisite to finding solutions in the ecosystem. Start-ups are typically very innovative and agile. Collaborating with start-ups can provide the acceleration larger or mature companies need to develop and introduce new technologies. We can find countless illustrations of this, for example in the area of data analytics or artificial intelligence where start-ups propose packaged solutions to enhance the data and propose services to improve predictability.

Universities are typically great partners for radical innovations. There are governmental programs that support such research and favor active participation from all stakeholders. There are such programs in most countries as well as in partnerships among countries. The European project OpenQKD—Open European Quantum Key Distribution—is one example of this type of research project toward radical innovation involving 38 partners—large enterprises, SMEs, academics, research and technology organizations, and national institutes—from 13 EU countries.

It is important to understand these different levels of innovation in order to not restrict ourselves as we think about innovation. As we can see, innovation opportunities are immense and certainly much needed to address sustainability challenges. Collaborations are key enablers to enhance existing technologies or bring new technologies to market. Stakeholder capability mapping is a prerequisite to forming such collaborations.

Systemic innovations

Looking for complementarities and partnerships in capabilities to address unmet needs is a first level of what I would call *systemic innovations* because they emerge from collaborations among ecosystem partners. There is yet a possibility to go further by approaching the needs in their interrelations. As explained earlier, sustainability needs and challenges are interrelated. Thus, it takes system thinking to more efficiently address sustainability needs. This system thinking gives its full sense to the ecosystem analysis.

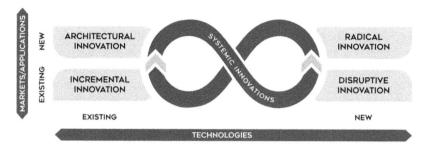

Figure 4.3 Systemic innovations.

Remember that ecosystem stakeholders are not limited to stakeholders on the value chain. If you don't look beyond the value chain, you may neglect some of your externalities and opportunities. A system thinking approach involves all stakeholders in the ecosystem, including the community, policymakers, and all adjacent players (Figure 4.3).

Considering how interrelated sustainability challenges are, this systemic approach to matching needs and capabilities becomes critical and a key accelerator to developing sustainable innovations. An example of this concerns energy management systems, which can be used for a group of energy users and self-producers of solar energy as well as for a variety of other uses. These systems implement the optimal match between different types of consumption—from lighting to electric vehicle charging—and electricity sources in order to encourage the use of renewable energies and decrease energy demand peaks. This is a win-win solution for the planet as it promotes solar energy production and for the finances of the users as self-produced energy is purchased at a lower price by distributors than energy from the grid and it decreases peak demand charges.

These systemic innovations can ultimately lead to innovative business models. One example that illustrates this in a commendable way is the challenge of mobility. The Geneva Climate Plan for 2030 has an objective to reduce by 5% to 10% the average kilometers traveled by motorized individual transport (MIT), reduce the number of remaining MIT trips by around 40% by shifting them to other modes of transport, and achieve an electrification rate (and/or equivalent technology) of around 40% of the remaining vehicle fleet. This will only be possible through systemic approaches. While public-private partnerships will be key to bringing the solutions needed, the efforts should actually go beyond these partnerships. Reaching such an objective will take great coordination from many actors, such as public transportation authorities, parking operators inside and outside cities, government policymakers, engaged city leaders, the real estate world, and obviously the inhabitants. Achieving this type of innovation thus goes beyond mapping capabilities. It requires looking for solutions to address the challenge in a systemic way. This systemic approach is also leading to new business models such as the sharing economy. For example, sharing bikes at train stations can be a way to promote train transportation for those who still need transportation for the so-called last kilometer.

Thus, systemic approaches enable us to develop the next level of innovation with potentially greater impact through new economic models. As explained in the first chapter, sustainability challenges require new economic models. We can highlight here a few innovative business models that can address systemic challenges:

- Circular economy: where the business models look at the entire life cycle of a product,
- Sharing economy: where we look at sharing products or services among users,
- Functionality economy: where we look at the functionality and use of a product versus possession,
- Shared value economy: where we are basically looking at sharing and growing the "pie" amongst stakeholders.

All these business models take a thorough ecosystem analysis and a system thinking approach and lead to systemic innovations. They can have a great positive impact as they address several unmet needs at their root and in a systemic and sustainable way. See Chapter 5 for a more in-depth discussion of new business models.

Leverage collective intelligence

To accelerate the transition to sustainable development, it is critical to not only involve but *engage* all stakeholders. When it comes to sustainable innovation, we see more and more practices in that direction. These practices leverage the power of collective intelligence.

Open sustainability innovation and marketing

Along the same lines of taking a systemic approach to identify the solutions we need, an excellent practice to deploy Positive Impact Marketing is the concept of *open innovation*.

A common definition for open sustainability innovation is "opening up the company, especially research and development, and involving different kinds of stakeholders into the development process of sustainable products and services."

The opportunity of this approach is huge, first, because it involves the consumer in the design of a solution, and second, because of the many different perspectives that are brought forth to a given need or opportunity.

Likewise, we now hear the term *open sustainability marketing*, which can be defined as "opening the company, notably its marketing, and involving different kinds of stakeholders in developing the marketing strategy of sustainable products and services."

The principle of open marketing is totally coherent with the systemic approach described in Positive Impact Marketing. It suggests engaging stakeholders and partners in each step of the marketing strategy development process, from environment analysis to understanding unmet needs and capabilities, defining value propositions, and developing communication strategies.

These open approaches bring forward the power of collective intelligence.

One doesn't need to be an expert to come up with a new solution. Actually, both expert and nonexpert views are valuable especially if the nonexpert view is from stakeholders and in particular end users. Open approaches gather a variety of stakeholders, each bringing a different perspective that can help develop new solutions to complex problems. The full power of open collaboration is exemplified by hackathons—events in which people with diverse backgrounds and expertise collaborate in a sprint lasting a few hours or a few days to create solutions and corresponding business models. We see more and more of these hackathons being run on different themes. Hackathons related to the theme of smart cities, for example, allow the inhabitants (hence, the primary stakeholders) to become involved. Experience has proven that open innovation in the field of smart cities can elicit many innovative ideas. In this approach, we look at involving a key stakeholder that has long been neglected. I would call this stakeholder the *very-end users*. They could be the inhabitants or citizens. They are the human stakeholders that are ultimately impacted at the very end of the life cycle of each product.

Prospective innovation

Besides hackathons, we see emerging forms of ideation such as design thinking. One that is promising, especially considering the uncertainty of our world as well as the challenges ahead, is *prospective innovation*. Prospective innovation involves focusing on exploring the future.

The idea is to start by defining the possible or desired future. Innovation will emerge on the path from the present to that desired future. Different scenarios are designed and assessed, leading to creative solutions. One engages in a paradigm shift in thinking through challenges.

As the Positive Impact Marketer looks to address sustainability challenges, defining the possible or desired future versus the probable future is certainly an easier exercise. Looking at the desired future is another way to engage the "very-end user." It is leveraging collective intelligence in the sense that here again, you open up possibilities along the entire life cycle of a product or situation.

One example of prospective innovation applied to product development is the Solar Impulse plane. Solar Impulse sought to resolve the challenge of building a plane that could go around the globe only using solar energy. It was only when they changed the paradigm and looked at the end in mind that they could solve the challenge. They switched from a logic of how to produce and store enough energy to fly around the globe, which proved unsolvable, to one of how to rethink the design of the plane so that it uses only the energy that can be produced by the sun during the flight. They then involved suppliers of each part of the plane to rethink its design with this end in mind. The prospective approach combined with a collaborative approach along the entire value chain enabled them to build a lighter plane that would use only the energy that could be produced flying around the world.

 Takeaway

Once unmet needs are identified, Positive Impact Marketers will define the unique capabilities of their companies, and, in a systemic approach to marketing, will look for complementary capabilities from eco-system players. The system thinking at play will enable to develop the systemic innovations we need to solve complex and interrelated sustainability challenges. Collective intelligence, in particular through open innovation and marketing, which encourages stakeholders from a variety of backgrounds to participate, will lead to greater positive impact solutions.

Testimony

Systemic innovation and collective intelligence to meet a complex challenge

Sabrina Cohen Dumani—Founder and CEO of Nomads Foundation
In an effort to resolve our planet's environmental challenges, in particular, through the reduction of greenhouse gas emissions and the fight against climate change, it is essential to develop clean mobility solutions. Low-carbon hydrogen offers a promising solution alternative to fossil fuels. The GOH! (Génération Hydrogène) project meets this need by exploring the economic and technical feasibility of an entirely local hydrogen supply chain, thus contributing to the three pillars of sustainable development: environmental, social, and economic.

This Swiss project involves five key players—Migros Genève, GreenGT, LARAG, SIG, and the Nomads Foundation—who are currently collaborating in a pilot project to construct a hydrogen-powered 40-ton truck. The collaboration unfolds as follows:

GreenGT: Specialized in electric-hydrogen propulsion, GreenGT contributes its technical expertise. GreenGT has developed the fuel cell and hydrogen propulsion powertrain (GMP) for the truck.

LARAG: A Swiss specialist in the construction of commercial and heavy-duty vehicles, LARAG plays a role in adapting vehicles for the integration of hydrogen propulsion. LARAG is currently building the vehicle designed by GreenGT.

SIG: Services Industriels de Genève (SIG), which provides essential services to the residents of Geneva including water, gas, electricity, and thermal energy, is responsible for the production of the green hydrogen that will power the truck.

Migros Genève: A key player in the retail sector that seeks to reduce its carbon footprint through sustainable logistics, Migros Genève will begin transporting its goods with the GoH! truck, thus testing the vehicle until it is fully available on the market.

Nomads Foundation: A catalyst for the project, the Nomads Foundation ensures synergy between the various players and the monitoring of systemic innovation, as well as the development of future workforce skills.

The "GOH!" project is an emblematic example of systemic innovation in sustainable mobility. The systemic approach begins with considering all the interdependent components of a problem. In the

GOH! project, this means recognizing the interactions between energy production, transport logistics, propulsion technologies, and environmental impacts. The Nomads Foundation plays a crucial role in orchestrating these different components, facilitating collaboration, and ensuring that collective efforts converge toward a common goal.

The GOH! project also exemplifies systemic innovation because it does not limit itself to incremental improvements in a single area; it transforms the entire mobility system. By integrating low-carbon hydrogen technologies into freight transport, the project is redefining the way energy is produced, distributed, and used, while considering the social and economic impacts.

The use of open marketing and open innovation techniques has been crucial to the project's success. By adopting an open approach, the project enables cross-disciplinary collaboration between companies, research institutions, and the public. Collective intelligence, involving the sharing of knowledge and skills between stakeholders, facilitates innovation and rapid adaptation to technical and operational challenges. Forecasting, for its part, helps to anticipate future market and training developments, as well as technological, economic, and environmental implications, thus guiding strategic decision-making.

The GOH! project aims to have a positive impact on the three pillars of sustainable development:

- Environmental: Significant reduction in CO_2 emissions and dependence on fossil fuels, thanks to the use of green hydrogen,
- Social: Creation of local jobs in the hydrogen sector, improving air quality, and raising awareness of sustainable mobility,
- Economic: Development of a new economic sector around hydrogen, with growth and innovation potential for Swiss companies.

In conclusion, the GOH! project is a model of systemic innovation, integrating various stakeholders and disciplines to meet a complex challenge. Using open marketing and innovation techniques, collective intelligence, and prospective, the project positions itself as a forerunner in the field of sustainable mobility. Its success will have positive repercussions not only on the environment, but also on social and economic aspects, illustrating the potential impact of such innovative initiatives within the framework of sustainable development.

 **Key steps**

Three steps *to* Connect Needs and Capabilities

STEP 1: Prioritize consumer needs to be addressed

- Starting from the ecosystem analysis and stakeholder mapping, identify and prioritize the most pressing needs toward greater net positive impact,
- Define a brand purpose that helps drive responsible consumption.

STEP 2: Match needs and capabilities

- Assess your unique capabilities to address unmet needs as well as the capabilities of all stakeholders,
- Identify straightforward opportunities to solve unmet needs,
- Identify partnership opportunities to deliver systemic innovations for greater impact.

STEP 3: Leverage collective intelligence

- Identify opportunities for open innovation and marketing,
- Shift the paradigm with prospective innovation.

Bibliography

Unilever Sustainable Living Plan Report. https://www.unilever.com/planet-and-society, 2010.

Chapter 5

Connect Beginning and Ends

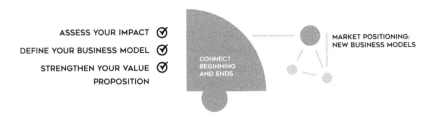

ASSESS YOUR IMPACT ☑
DEFINE YOUR BUSINESS MODEL ☑
STRENGTHEN YOUR VALUE ☑
PROPOSITION

CONNECT
BEGINNING
AND ENDS

MARKET POSITIONING:
NEW BUSINESS MODELS

Figure 5.1 Connect Beginning and Ends.

With this element, we now move from the market analysis and targeting phase to the market positioning part of strategic marketing. This element—Connect Beginning and Ends—is key to defining business models. We offer here an expanded perspective on product and service lifecycles, showing why the traditional "beginning" of a lifecycle is not necessarily the beginning and the "end" is not necessarily the end in terms of social and environmental impact. Understanding this entire life cycle of the product helps enhance the value proposition and business model toward greater positive impact (Figure 5.1).

As mentioned earlier, Positive Impact Marketing provides the framework to place a company within its business ecosystem, with consideration of all stakeholders. This ecosystem approach involves understanding externalities not only in space or with stakeholders but also in time. As mentioned in the definition of sustainability, it implies to "meet the needs of the present without compromising the ability of future generations to meet their own needs."

Thus, Positive Impact Marketing must look at the impact of a product and company on the next generations. This implies not only looking downstream but also gaining a thorough understanding upstream. To do that, the company will have to assess and manage the impact on the entire life cycle of each product. This element will be instrumental to ensure the

DOI: 10.4324/9781003422709-6

value proposition and business model does take into consideration the entire life cycle of the offering. Once the business model is defined, the Positive Impact Marketer will be able to optimize further the company's positive impact while refining the value proposition.

Impact management

Life cycle assessment

It is the responsibility of Positive Impact Marketing to ensure the footprint of the product and the company is assessed for its entire life cycle—which extends beyond the traditional parameters of a "product life cycle."

For example, many products are now made from recycled materials. The intention is certainly commendable. Yet, what about the impact across the entire life cycle? How do we ensure that the environmental impact of a recycling option of a given product will be net positive versus another option?

To answer this question more clearly, the marketer must perform the measurement of scope 1, 2, and 3 emissions of both direct and indirect greenhouse gases (GHG) described in Chapter 3. While scope 1 and scope 2 look at emissions during operations and energy supplies for operations, scope 3 looks at all emissions associated for which the company is *indirectly* responsible for, up and down its value chain. Scope 3 emissions are probably the most difficult to assess since they are outside of the company. One example of these emissions relates to the end-of-life treatment of sold products.

The methodology consisting of assessing the emissions throughout the entire life cycle of a product is called Life Cycle Assessment (LCA). The LCA is a key methodology used in Corporate Social Responsibility (CSR). An LCA assesses the environmental impact of a given product (or service) along its entire life cycle, including all the resources (e.g., raw or auxiliary materials) involved in the original production of the product to any impact of the product at the very end of life, including waste management or recycling. It is to be noted that because of the complexity of assessing scope 3, LCAs do not always cover the full breadth of scope 3 emissions. The Positive Impact Marketer will have to be careful to account for most of these scope 3 emissions beyond scopes 1 and 2. A thorough ecosystem analysis and stakeholder mapping will make it easier to identify these and at a minimum those with greatest impact.

Several companies or consultants perform such assessments. Using an external party ensures thoroughness of the assessment but also provides credibility. Creating trust and avoiding the perception of greenwashing is what the marketer must strive for here and this will be covered later in the book.

 **Definition**

Life Cycle Analysis (LCA) analyzes the negative impacts of products or services during their entire life cycle, from the moment it is produced to the period it is in use to end-of-life. LCA will cover all upstream processes (for example, the processes by suppliers in the creation of the product) and downstream processes (for example, processes to manage the product when it becomes waste) from production to end-of-life.

The International Organization for Standardization (ISO) offers guidelines for conducting an LCA according to ISO 14040 and 14044.

Reporting frameworks and organizations

In parallel to the work done by the UN toward sustainable development goals, we have seen an increasing importance of Environmental, Social, and corporate Governance (ESG) reporting for companies worldwide. This involves disclosures from companies on their environmental impacts, social impacts, and governance practices.

There exist a few organizations and frameworks that help businesses, governments, and other organizations understand and communicate their impact in areas such as climate change, human rights, and corruption. These organizations are very well known by the CSR structures within companies. Let's mention here a few of these that are very relevant for impact management. We'll mention here just a few of these.

The Global Reporting Initiative (GRI) is one of these frameworks. The sustainability reporting standards proposed (the GRI Standards) are widely used by organizations. They enable organizations to understand and report on their impacts on society and the environment in a consistent, transparent, and reliable way. This reporting is hence highly relevant to many stakeholders, including investors, capital markets, policymakers, and civil society. The methodology proposed is used by CSR leaders to perform nonfinancial reporting for their companies.

Another organization of reference is the Carbon Disclosure Project (CDP), a not-for-profit organization running the global disclosure system for organizations to manage their environmental impacts. Its focus is hence on environmental data and climate-related risks and opportunities. It offers advice on reporting and supports organizations in managing environmental risks. The CDP can thus be a great partner for Positive Impact Marketers as they look to assess and manage environmental impact for the products.

Another key initiative supporting ESG strategies of businesses is the Science Based Targets initiative (SBTi). SBTi is a collaboration between the CDP, the United Nations Global Compact, the World Resources Institute (WRI), and the World Wildlife Fund (WWF). This initiative established in 2015 has set targets that are science-based with a specific calculation methodology to reach net zero targets and climate goals. SBTi has been adopted by over 1000 companies to date, renowned brands, and NGOs and provides a reference or certification for positive environmental goals and claims.

These frameworks offer methodologies to complement the LCA in assessing and improving impact management. Initially designed to support governments and organizations and used by CSR leaders, they seem to be an essential tool for the Positive Impact Marketer to complement traditional marketing practices. For that reason, the Positive Impact Marketer will want to collaborate very closely with the CSR team when it comes to impact assessment. These frameworks also provide credibility and certifications that are essential to avoid greenwashing.

New business models

Beyond ensuring credibility, the LCA (or any other similar impact management exercise) is an excellent way to identify opportunities for mitigating the negative impact of products or services and striving for net positive impact. A straightforward example of mitigation is when it comes to the specification of a given product: the Positive Impact Marketer can spot the potential opportunity for substitute raw materials or natural ingredients that can enhance the ecological profile of the formulated product or its recyclability. Such opportunities will nourish the value proposition and business model.

The LCA can also help identify new business models, notably more circular business models. In traditional business models, products follow a linear lifecycle, at the end of which the product becomes a waste. In circular business models, the products don't become waste, but rather can become a resource for another product's lifecycle. The original product's lifecycle thus loops into other products' lifecycles, instead of ending abruptly. The LCA can support this circular effort by, for example, analyzing the "second life" of a used material at the end of its "first life." The complementary impact reporting activities will also enable to fine-tune the business model going beyond emissions impact and considering all other environmental and social impacts. For example, when considering the impact of a global business on local communities or biodiversity, the business model could be redesigned to include local partnerships.

Thus, while performing a full impact assessment, the Positive Impact Marketer can discover new business models.

Circular business models

A major new business model that supports sustainability is the circular business model. The circular economy is governed by 3Rs: Reduce, Reuse, and Recycle.

- **Reduce:**
  The first consideration here is: do we need to use a given product or could we propose a solution to either not use that product or use less of it? In terms of the transition to more sustainable energy, for example, before moving to "greener" or renewable sources of energy, one should consider how to primarily reduce the *use* of energy by looking for energy efficiency solutions. To successfully achieve the energy transition, it is key to keep in mind that the best energy is the one we do not use! This applies in many domains.

  Next consideration: how can the use of certain components of the product, or input used in the production process, such as energy or water, be reduced? This assessment can have a direct impact on the bottom line as well as bringing forth new opportunities. We mentioned earlier the example of dyeing systems in the textile industry that can help reduce both energy and water consumption.

- **Reuse:**
  What can be the destiny of raw materials used during the production process? How about the product itself? Can these be used for other purposes instead of being considered a waste? Developing countries where resources are scarce are experts at considering these questions. Every equipment typically has many different lives. In the textile industry, for example, the fabric in used clothing will have a second life or third life. We also see many initiatives that promote the reuse of materials through exchange forums or repair cafés.

  Another example of reuse occurs when parts of a product can find new uses after the product's end of life. This situation often arises when new technologies replace older ones. For example, how can existing manual electricity metering systems be repurposed when these are replaced with smart metering, which is happening in Switzerland as I write this. Or how smartphone producers can reuse parts of our smartphones when they reach their end of life? A good example of reusing part of a product when it becomes obsolete is the extraction and selling of the copper within electric cables once these cables need to be changed by electricity distribution companies for quality insurance purposes after their approved lifetime. Considering the cost of copper, such valorization of the copper is good for both the planet and the wallet!

• **Recycle:**
Can a product, after the end of its first life, be recycled to a second life? Can it become a resource for another purpose or another product of value? This is, to some extent, another form of reuse where parts of a product can be used to produce a new product. This consideration also allows the marketer to increase the life cycle of a given product and thus revisit the whole business model. There are quite a few examples of this today, especially in the cement industry. There is research going on to safely recycle plastic in cement production. Also, in the waste-water treatment process, where sludges, a byproduct of the water treatment process, can be used to produce biogas and as an alternative fuel or raw material to produce cement.

Considering these 3 Rs of circular economy, I would like to add a fourth R to it: Redesign.

• **Redesign:**
There is indeed an opportunity for the Positive Impact Marketer to take a more holistic approach to impact management from the very beginning, at the conception phase of the product, through its production, and toward its end of life.

Redesign entails rethinking the design and production process of a product at the early stage so that it can mitigate its negative impact or contribute to a more circular economy downstream. Such opportunities should be identified from the product conception phase.

A way to redesign a product is to look at the efficiency of the entire system. For example, high-performance lubricants used in the automotive industry help reduce emissions through reduced frictions and therefore reduced fuel consumption. Likewise, water retention solutions proposed in the agriculture sector help to reduce water consumption during the plant-growing phase.

Another way to apply the redesign mindset is to consider redesigning a product with the ability to be recycled as part of the product functionality. This is for example a key opportunity in the textile industry where not mixing several different raw materials to produce the fabric makes the recycling of the garment technically and financially possible or easier.

Considering these 4 Rs of the circular economy and using principles of LCA on scope 1, 2, and 3 emissions, one can redefine the business model integrating partners that will enable either of the 4 Rs. These will be called circular business models.

Regenerative business models

Along the lines of a circular economy, we now see more and more focus on regenerative business models. This focus includes systemic design of products in order not only to mitigate negative impact but target net positive impact. These models will strive to restore and improve natural and social systems rather than depleting or harming them.

In regenerative models, one will look to design products based on resources that are most available and which use has the lowest impact to the environment. This approach pays close attention to the planetary boundaries. It is very aligned to the objectives of Positive Impact Marketing in the sense that it promotes long-term thinking as well as collaboration with stakeholders to build resilient and sustainable systems.

We see more and more of this approach in the agricultural sector. An example would be the agroforestry industry looking to combine trees with crops or livestock in order to increase agricultural productivity, improve soil quality, and sequester carbon. Another example would be with renewable energy and energy communities, where the aim is to create a resilient and self-sustaining energy system maximizing the use of locally produced renewable energy such as solar panels.

Through its systemic approach and respect for social and environmental systems, the regenerative economy is a major consideration and aligned to the principles of Positive Impact Marketing.

Adjacent business models

Diving deeper into the concepts of the circular and regenerative business models, we can find adjacent business models. The sharing economy is one of these and is considered to be another key new business model towards sustainability.

In this case, we are looking to optimize the use of a product, either by reducing consumption or by favoring the reuse of a product. This approach has a very strong value proposition for goods that are underused by a target population. Take the example of tools for Do-It-Yourself (DIY) uses. There are a number of DIY tools that we may use very seldom. Hence looking for sharing solutions is more appropriate both from an environmental and financial point of views as we then reduce overall consumption. This approach can also help bring systemic solutions to solve sustainability challenges. Car sharing is a very good example of this.

Such offerings and business models can help decrease the overall footprint of mobility.

The sharing economy is also known as the collaborative economy or functionality economy. These business models are looking to encourage the use and functionality of a product collectively versus as the possession of an individual.

All these business models are great business models for the Positive Impact Marketer to consider. The exercises of connecting stakeholders and connecting needs and capabilities described in Chapters 3 and 4 combined with a holistic impact assessment will be great enablers to identify opportunities for such new business models. They help to Connect Beginning and Ends. We consider here two definitions of "ends": first in the sense of the final phase of the life cycle of the product, but also in terms of what is the *purpose* of the brand. Life cycle and purpose need to be connected.

 Takeaway

Impact management provides the marketer with purposeful and strategic questions to consider in the market positioning phase which can result in circular business or regenerative opportunities: How can companies prompt the consumer to reduce consumption while managing the impact on the business plan and profit/loss model? How shall we manage the end of life of a product? What partnerships can we form to integrate the reuse of our product in the business model? How can a product be designed for recyclability? Such a mindset enables the marketer to re-think existing business models and identify potential new sustainable business models and define a positive brand purpose.

Grounding your business model: The value proposition

Just as with traditional marketing, the marketer must thoroughly define the value proposition of the product or service offered. Defining the value proposition is key to ensuring the profitability of a business. Let's not forget that profit is one of the fundamental Ps in the 3Ps of sustainable development.

It is only by ensuring that a business can sustain itself that we will be able to establish a viable economic model. This is often the challenge to which social entrepreneurs are confronted. As they want to focus mainly on social and environmental aspects with an aversion for profit, they tend to fall into the trap of not positioning their business model to extract the necessary financial value so that it can be sustainable and actually increase its positive impact.

 Definition

A **value proposition** captures benefits that customers receive from buying and using a product or service. The benefits can range from utilitarian (customers are able to do what they want to do), economic (customers receive the utilitarian benefit of the product for a lower price), or emotional (the product fulfills the customers' emotional needs).

Defining a value proposition is central to any business model and strategic marketing. In Positive Impact Marketing, this exercise will have to be more holistic and take into consideration the entire ecosystem, all stakeholders, and the life span of the product while ensuring the business model operates within social and planetary boundaries.

Creating a value proposition starts with the definition of "value." The Positive Impact Marketer will consider not only financial value but equally, if not more, social and environmental value. He will do that with the entire life cycle in mind. We hear more and more the idea of "creating value from values" which says it all. This approach has broad implications for the value proposition. One concerns the evaluation of cost. The Positive Impact Marketer should look to assess the total cost of products and services. This assessment must include not only the cost to produce and deliver but also the direct and indirect cost of use and post-use. The cost of use will include for example environmental impacts due to transportation. The cost of post-use will include waste management costs. Also, from a social perspective, the analysis should factor in the behavior you want to create—which raises the question of how sustainable behavior and solutions are rewarded and made easier to acquire.

The Real, Win, Worth (RWW) screen can be an easy tool to use to develop a business model that factors in all aspects of sustainability. It has originally been developed by Dominick M. Schrello to be used in early stage of the innovation process (Figure 5.2).

The RWW methodology is very intuitive yet comprehensive. It is commonly used in strategic marketing approaches and has been around for a while. It is a great tool to ground the business model and strengthen the value proposition. The marketer will go through key questions to

Figure 5.2 The RWW screen.

define if and to what extent the market is "Real" both in terms of market attractiveness and technical feasibility, whether the company can "Win" with the offering considering product differentiation and synergies with core competencies and, finally, what is the "Worth" of the offering or business modeling terms of strategic alignment as well as risk/reward ratio.

The Positive Impact Marketer should add critical sustainability considerations to this RWW methodology, such as externalities, LCA, or partnership opportunities (Figure 5.3). To guarantee a sustainable business model based on a solid value proposition, he can expand the RWW as follows:

- **Is the market REAL?** This analysis will have to be complemented with elements brought forward in the ecosystem analysis. In particular, this analysis will assess the alignment of the business model with sustainability-related megatrends, contributions to SDGs, social and environmental externalities, or impact on stakeholders. The analysis will also need to make sure the business model is focused on the most pressing needs for society and the planet,
- **Can we WIN?** This analysis will have to include considerations for stakeholders and complementarities; what impactful partnerships can we form? It should also make sure to add an impact assessment through the entire life cycle of the product,
- **What is the product's WORTH?** In this analysis, the value will have to be assessed beyond just financial value to include social and

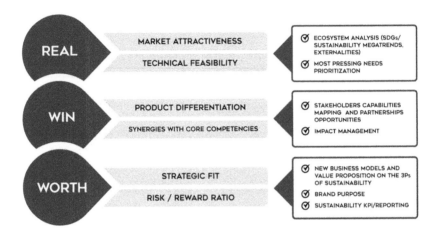

Figure 5.3 The positive impact RWW screen.

environmental value. It will have to consider new business model opportunities from the impact assessment. Then the analysis should be completed with an assessment of the brand purpose impact and its consistency across products and company activities. This element relates to our other interpretation of "end," meaning the purpose (as opposed to end of the life cycle) of the product. The brand purpose becomes a key consideration for the worth of the product. Finally, Key Performance Indicators (KPIs) related to sustainability reporting will need to be included.

The RWW methodology is a great tool to prioritize opportunities. One can set criteria for each element to perform such prioritization. As criteria are related to sustainability criteria, they can be powerful tools to prioritize opportunities that will offer the greatest positive impact. Thus, the Positive Impact Marketer can fine-tune and strengthen the value proposition for greater positive impact.

 Takeaway

Traditional tools of marketing can be used to define the value proposition and the business model. Yet they must be adjusted in scope to integrate environmental and social value for the whole life cycle of the product and business. Thus, Positive Impact Marketing can establish solid sustainable value propositions and business models.

Testimony

Introducing the circular economy to the Swiss luxury market

Nicolas Freudiger—Co-founder and CEO of ID Genève Watches

The Swiss luxury watch and jewelry industry is not known for its attention to sustainability issues or its transparency regarding how its activities impact the environment. ID Genève has a completely opposite approach, putting sustainability at the heart of its business strategy and culture. From the beginning, we wanted to enter the Swiss luxury market with a business model, and more than that, an *identity* built around the circular economy.

One fundamental way we achieve this is through the criteria we use to select suppliers, which are short routes, the carbon impact of materials, and the price of watch components. For example, the stainless steel in our watches comes from the waste of 40 watch-making companies in the Jura region of Switzerland and nearby areas. We are the only brand to use this surplus in its production of watches. It is local and traceable. Our LCA demonstrates that our 100% stainless steel is 10 times less impactful (CO_2) than industry average.

The metal for our watch cases is remelted down in a solar furnace, which reduces the carbon footprint of this process. For the collection Circular S, our Solar recycled stainless steel is 165 times less impactful (CO_2) than industry average.

We also have replaced the use of leather—which is harmful to the environment in many ways, including significant water usage and waste—with a substitute called Treekind™, which is plastic-free, estimated carbon neutral, and completely recyclable. When the leather straps are returned by customers they are turned into biogas (10 kg of organic waste produces 1 m³ of biogas). The result is a circular lifetime product cycle. Downcycle, we don't extract raw material but instead upcycle green waste (in the form of Treekind™) to manufacture the strap; eventually, once the strap is no longer being worn, it is recycled into biogas.

The cork Tencel™ fabric lining of the strap, which we source from the Swiss company Ono, is equally sustainable. Ono does not incorporate any polyester or plastic in its fabric and uses only water-based glue and water-based finishing, avoiding the harmful components of synthetic glue and finishing.

Another sustainable source of material for our products is the biomaterial, based on the waste from winemaking, which is produced by the Italian company Vegea.

Our efforts start even before sourcing and production since the design of our products is driven by sustainability considerations. A circular economy requires products designed to ensure a long product life cycle that reduces waste. We achieve this by taking a modular approach to the design of our products. For example, the side additions, dials, and bracelets of our watches can be changed at any time. This modular approach also promotes a long product life cycle through our business strategy, which is not based on presenting new collections every year, but instead offering annual updates of the existing collection.

The long product life cycle is further supported, on the service side, through our innovative use of what we call "circular tokens." The process works as follows: A portion of the customer's purchase price is set aside and converted into digital currency, which is then returned to the customer for use in our service department. Customers thus have access to free repairs of their watches, including the free replacement of parts. We hope this will encourage customers to maintain their watches.

Our circular approach to services is accessible to customers through the three service pillars of our digital platform: (1) traditional servicing; (2) modular servicing, with the replacement of parts; (3) refurbishment of watches that customers want to sell to the community or sell back to us.

Through our 100% commitment to sustainability and the circular manufacturing and servicing of our products, we are positioning ID Genève Watches at the forefront of a paradigm shift in the industry to the circular economy.

Key steps

Three steps *to* Connect Beginning and Ends

Step 1: Assess your impact

- Perform an LCA for your product or service considering scope 1, 2, and 3 emissions,
- Collaborate with the CSR team and use the global reporting frameworks to fine-tune and validate your impact assessment.

STEP 2: Define your business model

- Using the LCA, identify opportunities to define your business model considering the 3Rs of a circular economy: Reduce, Re-use, Recycle,
- Look for opportunities to Redesign (the 4th R) your product or business model towards a more circular or regenerative economic model.

STEP 3: Strengthen your value proposition

- Assess the strength of your value proposition considering not only financial but also social and environmental value,
- Define the Real-Win-Worth matrix applied to your offering and business model and integrate sustainability considerations (externalities, impact management, sustainability KPIs …),
- Refine your business model and value proposition using this adjusted RWW methodology and prioritizing a greater positive impact.

Bibliography

ISO 14040. Environmental Assessment—Life Cycle Assessment. https://www.iso.org/standard/37456.html, 2006.

Chapter 6

Connect Say and Do

DEFINE THE MARKETING MIX ✓

SET SMART; OBJECTIVES ✓

BUILD TRUST WITH YOUR BRAND ✓
PURPOSE

CONNECT
SAY AND
DO

MARKETING MIX &
CONTROL PLAN

Figure 6.1 Connect Say and Do.

Many people tend to associate marketing with communication. This is indeed, and I should say, unfortunately, how marketing has positioned itself for decades in a focused effort to push sales. Hopefully by now, you are convinced that there is much more to marketing—and in fact the opportunity for marketing to dramatically impact the world of global business is huge. However, as marketing looks to actually transform business models towards sustainability, it will have to be focused on building trust. This last part of the **Connect 4 Impact** methodology addresses the marketing mix and control plan. This is where all elements developed in the strategic marketing phase come together moving to implementation. This is also where it will be critical to align "Say" and "Do" in order to thoroughly operationalize the positive impact strategy and build trust (Figure 6.1).

Define the marketing mix

The strategic marketing phase in Positive Impact Marketing has been strengthened through the three first elements of the **Connect 4 Impact** methodology: Connect Stakeholders, Connect Needs and Capabilities, and Connect Beginning and Ends. This methodology has helped broaden the scope of the typical steps of strategic marketing adding considerations that are essential to establishing a sustainable business model.

DOI: 10.4324/9781003422709-7

With the last element looking to strengthen the positive impact value proposition, the marketer is ready to move to the marketing mix exercise, which will operationalize the strategy.

The objective now will be to break down the strategy into its key operational elements. As explained in Chapter 2, the recommendation is to keep only 4Ps for the marketing mix as other sustainability considerations have been integrated in the strategic marketing part and thus in the value proposition.

Let's come back to these 4Ps and see how they are positively influenced by the enhanced strategic marketing phase:

- **Product: What we offer**
  The offering of the company will now be strongly influenced by the strategic exercise of identifying stakeholders and potential externalities as well as complementarities. The offering will be refined to mitigate negative impacts or, better, enhance positive impacts on stakeholders. Complementarities will help refine the offering from the company relative to other stakeholders and looking for impactful partnerships.

  The understanding of most pressing needs and connecting them with capabilities will be essential to refine that offering.

  The assessment of the impact on the life cycle as well as new business models will help define how the product can be designed for sustainability or which offering fits the new business model.

  Thus, the strategic marketing phase while addressing these key considerations will provide the necessary input to ensure that the offering is defined with positive impact as a central consideration.

- **Price: What value we create for the user**
  This element will be defined from the value proposition and business model in order to determine what value is created for the user. It will have to include considerations from the stakeholder mapping and impact management to integrate elements of total cost to society. This cost to society will be assessed through the analysis of externalities and the life cycle assessment. The enhanced Real, Win, Worth analysis will also provide all necessary elements to define the right price.

- **Place: How we make it available**
  This element will be influenced by stakeholder partnerships as well as by the business model and value proposition. The new circular or regenerative business models will bring further consideration in terms of how to make the product available to the customer or how to handle its "end of life."

- **Promotion: How we share the value proposition**
  This element will be strongly influenced by the stakeholder mapping as well as the business model and positioning objective for each target segment. As we will see later in this section, creating a solid brand purpose that is consistent across the entire company and activities will be essential to build the trust needed. All promotion activities will have to be consistent and convey this brand purpose.

Therefore, the marketing mix exercise in Positive Impact Marketing will be very similar to the process in traditional marketing. What will be key though is that it be fully aligned to the input from the strategic marketing phase of the marketing strategy process, itself complemented by the **Connect 4 Impact** methodology.

This is the first consideration in connecting Say and Do where "Say" relates to the strategic intent—as defined in the strategic marketing phase—and "Do" to the operationalization of the strategy through the marketing plan.

However, in order to ensure that the Positive Impact Marketer actually connects this "Say" and "Do" over time, the control plan will be critical. The control plan is where objectives will be set and followed through over time.

Set "SMART*i*" objectives

As mentioned earlier, marketing has long been accused of manipulation and promoting false information. With Positive Impact Marketing, we are looking to firstly deliver net positive impact and secondly, create trust with stakeholders. Therefore, having a set of well pre-defined and comprehensive objectives is required.

Management by objectives is typically used in project management as well as human resource development and performance management. The SMART model, one of the most-used models for setting objectives, was first developed by George T. Doran in 1981 and sets out five characteristics—specific, measurable, actionable, realistic, and timebound—that make an objective "SMART." Originally, the model was used to identify the objectives of a project, whether qualitative or quantitative, over a given period. Simple yet effective, the SMART model, when applied in the right way, helps managers set clear goals that outline exactly what needs to be accomplished, and when. Considering the need for clarity and commitment over time for impact marketing, this is a very appropriate method to set impact marketing objectives (Figure 6.2).

Figure 6.2 SMART goals.

SMART objectives must be:

- **S—Specific:** Be clear and precise. That means concrete, detailed, and well-defined so that you know where you are going and what to expect when you arrive.
- **M—Measurable:** Numbers and quantities provide means of measurement and comparison. These measures must be reliable and preferably assessed by an external accredited organization as discussed in the prior section. The Positive Impact Marketer will look for recognized third-party certifications. They should support a measurable impact.
- **A—Actionable:** Feasible and easy to put into action. The Positive Impact Marketer should be able to track progress toward these goals and take corrective action as needed. Monitoring progress will be essential to guarantee impact as well as avoid false claims.
- **R—Realistic:** Considers constraints such as resources, personnel, cost, and time frame. Considering sustainability challenges, it is important for Positive Impact Marketers to have ambitious and audacious yet achievable and realistic goals.
- **T—Time-bound:** With a given time frame and clear deadlines. While sustainability and sustainable businesses look at the long-term aspects and impacts as opposed to the focus of most traditional businesses on the short term, it is critical to set objectives not only for the short and medium term but, just as importantly, for the long term.

Hence the impact marketer will have to define SMART objectives. While this is a guarantee towards impact measurement, the Positive Impact Marketer should make sure to include a broader scope for impact. While traditional marketing is very focused on economic or financial impact, the Positive Impact Marketer will have to look for a broader positive impact.

The suggestion here is to build on SMART objectives' proven approach to objective management but add a sixth element—"impactful"—for the Positive Impact Marketer. We'll refer here to the SMART*i* objectives.

SET GOALS ON THE 3Ps OF SUSTAINABILITY: PEOPLE – PLANET – PROFIT

Figure 6.3 The SMARTi goals.

- *i*—**Impactful**: The Positive Impact Marketer will look at the net impact of the product on its life cycle and towards all stakeholders. Beyond mitigating negative impacts, he will strive for net positive impact. He will also have to ensure that all these objectives consider the three pillars of sustainability: People, Planet, and Profit—where profits should be directed to further serving People and Planet (Figure 6.3).

Thus, the Positive Impact Marketer will have ecological and social objectives as well as economic objectives. As mentioned earlier, the value proposition must be based on a consideration for value that goes beyond economics to include environmental and social aspects. Let's look more closely at each of these three sets of objectives (Figure 6.4).

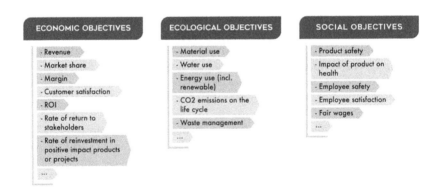

Figure 6.4 SMARTi objectives on the three pillars of sustainability.

Economic objectives

Economic objectives have been the most used in the history of marketing. They include indicators such as revenue, margin, market share, and customer satisfaction. One can argue that customer satisfaction should rather be considered as a social indicator, especially in a sustainable business model. Considering that the notion of the "customer" involves a revenue stream and is essential to revenues, customer satisfaction could also fall under economic objectives. That said, the customer is also a key stakeholder in society. Therefore, depending on the nature of the business, the customer satisfaction indicator could be either an economic or social indicator.

While economic objectives are common to most traditional businesses, they are the ones with which social entrepreneurs typically struggle the most. Indeed, these entrepreneurs make a point to have strong claims on social and environmental objectives. While this is commendable, their focus on social and environmental objectives is often at the expense of economic objectives and thus profitability. Yet if these businesses aspire to become sustainable and have a real impact today and tomorrow, it is critical that economic objectives be in place. It is only by ensuring that they can self-fund themselves and their growth that these businesses will ensure a positive impact in the long run. For example, a social entrepreneur who offers a product with high positive impact on the environment but doesn't ensure a certain profitability in its business model will probably either not survive or be preoccupied with looking for grants instead of effectively running the business. The whole point with profits is how they are being used. Are they shared with all stakeholders or just benefit a few shareholders? To what extent are they reinvested in the business in a way that makes a positive contribution to society and the planet? These should be metrics for the Positive Impact Marketer to consider and add to the traditional economic metrics.

Social objectives

These objectives include indicators for employees such as employee safety and wellness, employee satisfaction, inclusion and diversity, and fair wages. They also include indicators for the community and in consideration of the externalities of the product. Social indicators are traditionally corporate indicators. Yet if a business wants to transform the business models towards a sustainable model, it is key that those indicators be considered at the product or service level and hence by the Positive Impact Marketer.

When applied at the product level, such indicators could include product safety during use or impact of product on health.

By having these indicators at the product or service level, we can ensure the consistency in sustainability claims that is required. Take fair wages for example; the marketer designing the solutions or forming partnerships along the value chain must integrate the fair wage objective into the design of the product through the selection of partners and raw materials. A company cannot claim fair wages in its CSR engagement and then not apply "fair wages" at the product level. We'll come back to the aspect of consistency and building credibility later in the chapter. Thus, "fair wages" should be set as an objective at the product level, incorporating the entire supply chain.

Environmental objectives

Environmental objectives could include indicators such as material use, water use, energy consumption, emissions on the life cycle, or waste management. As just explained for social objectives, it is key that these objectives be integrated in the design of the product and production process and fully consistent with company objectives. These should be set, measured, and tracked at the product level.

 Takeaway

Positive Impact Marketers must fully align the marketing mix to the strategic marketing steps themselves completed with the **Connect 4 Impact** methodology. Once the marketing mix is defined, it will be key to define objectives that are SMART*i*: Specific, Measurable. Actionable, Realistic, Time-bound, as well as *i*mpactful. Further consideration shall be focused on gaining third-party certification, setting ambitious yet realistic goals, or focusing on the short and medium as well as longer term. They must strive for net positive impact on economic, environmental, and social aspects. These objectives will guide the control plan.

Build trust with your brand purpose

With the rise of green marketing, we have also seen an increase in the incidences of greenwashing. Consumers have immediate access to more information than ever before and have become more informed and discerning in product selection. This is good news for sustainability marketing. Consumers can more easily review and investigate product claims and reduce greenwashing as companies cannot hide behind false or exaggerated claims. Consumer awareness and activism thus serve Positive Impact Marketing.

To build trust, companies and Positive Impact Marketers will have to build credibility. Credibility is a key if not unique way to counter greenwashing. Trust and credibility are essential to establish a strong brand purpose. The brand purpose is the commitment of the company through all its brands to support people and planet. This notion may have been followed lightly by traditional marketers making easy claims and leading to greenwashing. Establishing a solid brand purpose is critical for the Positive Impact Marketer. It will indeed enable the necessary consistency with company's purpose and offer a guarantee for positive impact.

There are a few key principles that the Positive Impact Marketer will have to observe to establish credibility and thus trust with the brand's purpose.

Align actions and stated objectives

As explained earlier, the Positive Impact Marketer shall focus on establishing sustainable business models at the initial step of strategic marketing. However, once the strategic objectives have been delineated into SMART*i* goals, it will be critical to align the entire marketing mix with these goals and set a control plan.

Thus, it will be critical to:

- Review your marketing mix to ensure consistency with stated SMART*i* goals.
  Each of the traditional 4Ps of the marketing mix should reflect these commitments, whether it is for the product itself, the price, the promotion, or the way to market or place. Let's take the example of price, which is probably the least straightforward. Economic objectives should include value not only in terms of profit but for society and for the planet. The cost should consider the cost of production, use as well as the impact of post-use cost on profit, society, and planet.
- Develop a control plan that will guarantee consistency and impact.
  Just like in traditional marketing, the Positive Impact Marketer will have to develop a control plan. While this practice is not always thoroughly conducted in traditional marketing, it will be critical to establish credibility and trust for the Positive Impact Marketer. The SMART*i* objectives will be used to develop this control plan and follow through over time.

Guarantee reliability and transparency

There are more and more organizations providing impact measurement services. Not only do they bring expertise in impact measurement, but they also provide certification for these assessments. This guarantees the reliability of claims and information.

Another way to guarantee reliability and transparency is using labels on products. However, we are seeing an exponential rise of labels, many of which have no official certification tied to them. While the use of labels is an excellent way to prove claims made, one must be very selective about the labels being used.

Partnerships with NGOs are another source to guarantee reliability. These organizations can provide connections to networks and movements such as the Science Based Targets initiative (SBTi) as well as organizations that can provide certified impact measurements. This relates to reporting which has been covered under the impact management section earlier.

Ensure consistency

As mentioned earlier, it is essential that the marketing strategy for a product or service be fully consistent with other marketing actions related to that product or service. It is equally important that the same consistency be seen across products as well as with the strategy of the company itself. Thus, consistency must be seen across the product line, throughout the company, and over time.

To achieve this, all scorecards must be aligned. The SMARTi goals for a given product must be consistent across all products of that company and with the scorecard of the company.

For a business to be recognized as consistent in sustainability practices, not only the strategy but the culture of the company must also be aligned. This means that all employees are to understand and embody the mission and objectives of the company. Employees and leaders, starting with the CEO, must walk the talk of the company's sustainability claims.

Finally, the values of the company and its "raison d'être" must reflect the commitments. We mentioned earlier the importance of aligning the brand purpose of a product to the purpose of the company. Thus, all activities and measurements from the Positive Impact Marketer should be aligned and consistent with the brand purpose and the company purpose.

Takeaway

With the rise of greenwashing, building trust is essential for the Positive Impact Marketer. This is achieved first by aligning all actions to stated strategic claims and objectives. Trust and credibility can be reinforced through observing key principles: reliability, transparency, and consistency. The objective for the Positive Impact Marketer in the implementation phase will be to establish a strong brand purpose that will contribute to building trust with the company and its offering toward positive impact.

 Testimony

Using collective intelligence to increase transparency and reliability with impact assessment

Bertrand Gacon—Co-Founder and CEO Impaakt, Initiator of project SwiSOX (Swiss Social Stock Exchange) by SFG (Sustainable Finance Geneva), Programme co-director SDG Investing Certificate at the Geneva Graduate Institute, Former Head of Corporate Sustainability Lombard Odier Group.

One of the ways that we as individuals can have a major impact on sustainability is through the companies in which we invest, in our pension funds for example. The challenge is to know which companies are truly making a positive social, environmental, and economic impact. Which companies are really doing what they say they are doing? That's where *Impaakt* steps in. Through a collaborative platform that uses the power of collective intelligence, we document, analyze, and assess the impact of companies on the planet and society, and summarize our findings in an impact score.

The innovative process we use engages and involves all the company's stakeholders, and civil society as a whole, in assessing the materiality of its impacts. Of course, the challenge with crowdsourcing impact scores is to make sure the scores are based on rigorous research. We ensure this rigorous research through a call-for-contributions engine that defines the entire list of impact topics to be covered for a given company. Certified Impact Analysts reserve the topics they wish to research and write about, and submit their articles on the platform for review. Once all the quality criteria have been met, particularly with regard to sources, the analysis is validated and published online. It can then be read by all our 55,000 participants, who assess how positive/negative the impact is, and how material it is for the planet.

Every analysis published on the platform undergoes a thorough validation process to ensure that every piece of information is verified. This is key to ensuring that participants base their impact assessments on facts and figures, not perceptions. Next, we check the consistency and relevance of the ratings submitted. Our AI algorithms have been trained to detect any suspicious rating patterns or attempts at manipulation, and remove them immediately from the scoring system. We also give more weight to experienced and knowledgeable raters who have a proven track record in specific topics or industries.

For companies to change for the better, we need solid impact assessments that all participants can trust. Transparency is a key ingredient of this trust. Opaque and proprietary impact measurement methods often elicit criticism or accusations of greenwashing from civil society. And mistrust is the best recipe for inaction. Allowing everyone to participate in the impact assessment process is the best way to create the acceptability we need to change collectively.

Since our founding in 2018, we have amassed more than 1 million environmental and social assessments, from which we have created granular impact scores for more than 5,000 companies. The success of this approach is evident by the response we have received from investors in the company; up to now, that is, the fall of 2023, we have received $10 million in four rounds of funding.

Personally, I have created and led sustainable investment teams at several major banks over the past 20 years. My main lesson is that deep and radical change—the kind of change we need today—takes time and requires bringing together all stakeholders. You can't change finance (or business in general) by changing bankers alone. You change business by getting civil society on board. That's why we've decided to create a global collaborative sustainability resource, made by everyone, for everyone. If you want to go fast, go alone. If you want to go far, go together.

Key steps

Three steps *to* Connect Say and Do

Step 1: Define the marketing mix

- Align all tactics for each of the 4Ps to the prior strategic marketing steps,
- Ensure alignment of these tactics with each of the first three **Connect 4 Impact** elements.

Step 2: Set SMART*i* objectives

- To align "Say" and "Do," make sure that you have objectives for your marketing strategy that are SMART: Specific, Measurable, Actionable, Realistic, Time Bound. To guarantee positive impact, make sure they are also *i*mpactful, with positive impact on stakeholders over time and across the three pillars of sustainability: People, Planet, Profit.

Step 3: Build trust with your brand purpose

- Align actions to stated objectives: Ensure the marketing mix is aligned with SMART*i* goals, and a control plan guarantees consistency,
- Guarantee reliability and transparency of your claims with the help of recognized labels or certifications,
- Partner within the organization to ensure consistency across the company and to strengthen and align your brand and company purpose.

Chapter 7

Accelerating progress

The concept of sustainability is a simple one and is generally under-stood to be the securing of needs for today and for the future. What is difficult to grasp, particularly for a business enterprise, is how to make a positive impact and, most importantly, how to integrate the positive impact in the business model itself. The social and environmental challenges related to sustainability are not dismissed as catchphrases or temporary trends. However, what does sustainability really mean for business? "We already do a lot," many claim. "What shall we be doing differently?" "Can we really transform businesses, so they become sustainable?" "Is sustainability and business not antinomic per nature?"

Hopefully, this book has provided you with the tools to integrate sustainability at the core of the business model and strategy. It has helped you understand that making profit is not so much the issue. The question is rather about the ratio of these profits and what we are doing with it. Is a company extracting huge profits for the benefit of a few—the shareholders—or is it looking to create both social and environmental value for a broader base of stakeholders?

The urgency is here. Yet businesses are struggling to move to action at an accelerated pace and scale. There remain a number of barriers to action. How can we remove these barriers? Obviously, the answers to this question are broad and complex. And so are the roadblocks.

Removing roadblocks

In this chapter, we will have a quick look at the roadblocks to sustainable action specific to business management. The intent is not to analyze them in depth but rather to increase awareness so that one can relate to them when applying the concepts of the **Connect 4 Impact** methodology.

DOI: 10.4324/9781003422709-8

A necessary paradigm shift

The systemic approach and **Connect 4 Impact** framework covered in the previous chapters gave some insights on the "how" to transform a business into a sustainable and positive impact business. To accelerate this transformation, a total paradigm shift in how we do business is needed. This paradigm shift must happen from both an internal and an external perspective of the business itself.

From an internal perspective, the core issue is the role of business in society. The capitalist pursuit of making profit can no longer be the sole responsibility of businesses. Each business should redefine its purpose for being. And this purpose must incorporate social and environmental objectives to which the entire company strategy is aligned.

From an external perspective, the issue can be summarized with the following question: What is the impact a company wants to have on its environment and stakeholders? Reference has already been made to support the argument that a company can no longer be seen in isolation but rather placed into "its world"; meaning as an entity amongst all its stakeholders, which includes the planet itself. The defining of this raison d'être from an external perspective—that is, its reason for existing as manifested in its impact on the world—is the driver for the company mission and corresponding strategy. Along these lines, we see a growing trend towards *inclusive capitalism* within the Western capitalism, a movement that seeks to create long-term value that benefits all stakeholders. This is a huge paradigm shift which takes time to carry out. Such a shift is easier to achieve for small to medium-sized, local businesses. Such enterprises can evolve more quickly as they are more connected with their local environment. Also, the connection across internal functions is more closely knit, which facilitates the considerations of all aspects of the company strategy—as opposed to larger, more complex organizations that can operate in silos. In smaller companies, the marketer is typically working very closely with the purchaser, the human resource manager, any form of sustainability position that may exist, and, most importantly, the general manager or owner. This interface helps link the many different considerations to be taken when developing a sustainable business strategy, making system thinking and approach easier to achieve. While small and medium enterprises have great potential to lead the way, the transformation of our economic system cannot happen at scale without large businesses and corporations getting on board.

There are actions within the control of the marketer in traditional business and larger organizations that can be taken to accelerate change. Marketers can drive the transformation from within the organization through the **Connect 4 Impact** methodology—connecting the many dots internally and externally to ensure that sustainability is embedded in the business model with a strong link to the corporate strategy. Marketing has long been considered as a function located toward the end of the internal value chain. Positive Impact Marketing must be more central to the company's activities to enable a deep transformation.

As such this is a significant paradigm shift not only in how the company positions itself within its environment but also in redefining the roles within the company, starting with the role of marketing. This evolution requires a totally new mindset across the company.

The economic and financial system

In parallel to this company-level paradigm shift, another hurdle slowing the transformation to more sustainable business activities is the current economic system itself that rewards business performance based on financial impact and still not so much on non-financial impacts. Today, a company's profit and loss statement (P&L) always measures impact on financial capital but does not include impacts on environment, society, and stakeholders. The economic system is evolving thanks to the emergence of non-financial reporting and sustainable finance. ESG reporting is becoming a must for most organizations. Yet most performance metrics are still primarily financial and value short-term performance. The economic system still fails to evaluate performance on all aspects of sustainability and looking both at the short- and long-term impacts. We are still in a shareholder economy with quick benefits to a few and not in a stakeholder economy considering short and longer-term externalities.

As described earlier in the book, for sustainable development to occur, key performance indicators must assess not only economic performance but also environmental performance and social impact. And all three of these indicators should be assessed equally. Impact assessment methodologies and tools do exist and were introduced in Chapter 4 including CDP (Carbon Disclosure Project), SBTi (Science Based Targets initiative), and GRI standards, to name a few. Those are instrumental to ESG reporting. Actually, we see a number of reporting initiatives that, although promising, are also part of the problem in that they are still disconnected and lack uniformity. Impact measures and assessment expertise continue to emerge to fill this gap and adoption of these metrics is growing. Unfortunately, we are still missing one universal way of assessing impact on all three dimensions of performance recognized by the financial system. To avoid greenwashing and build the necessary trust mentioned earlier in the book, it is critical that these measures be consistent, transparent, and thus reliable. In that sense, the European Union is working on a taxonomy so that we use a single set of definitions and measurements. The EU taxonomy for sustainable activities is a classification system that defines criteria for economic activities that are aligned with a net zero trajectory by 2050 and its broader environmental goals other than climate. For example, the EU Commission's sustainable finance experts proposed biodiversity criteria for fishing and crop production, circular economy criteria for the construction and renovation of buildings, pollution prevention criteria for the finishing of textiles, and water preservation criteria for urban wastewater treatment.

Consistency across companies is critical to accelerate progress. For financial markets to broaden their valuation of company performance, uniform and credible assessment metrics for environmental and social impact must be established. The opportunity exists to establish uniformity and credibility in assessing environmental and social impact. There are a few initiatives in that direction, such as the most recent step forward from the International Sustainability Standard Board (ISSB). Mid 2023, the ISSB has issued its inaugural International Financial Reporting Standards (IFRS)—IFRS S1 General Requirements for Disclosure of Sustainability-related Financial Information and IFRS S2 Climate-related Disclosures—ushering in a new era of sustainability-related disclosures in capital markets worldwide. The standards create a common language for disclosing the effect of climate-related risks and opportunities, and will help to improve trust and confidence in company disclosures about sustainability to inform investment decisions. At the same time, they are consistent with existing standards such as the Global Reporting Initiative (GRI), The Task Force on Climate-Related Financial Disclosures (TCFD), or the European Sustainability Reporting Standards (ESRS). While the new ISSB standards represent an important step, there is still a way to go to achieve the needed comprehensive and unified global disclosure system.

Another consideration that is key to sustainable development, beyond the scope of impact on economic, environmental, and social aspects, is the timeframe involved. Besides rewarding economic performance primarily, our financial system also focuses more on short-term performance. A short-term view conflicts with the very essence of sustainability, which is to create positive and *sustained* change. Longer-term approaches support innovation and social practices—and depending on the industry, research for innovation can take from one to ten years or more. To support sustainable innovation, time is needed to bring innovations from ideation to market. Given the short-term financial metrics of the current economic model, innovation or strategic initiatives are put aside during downturns in the economic cycle. A strategic and consistent focus is required to see the longer-term impacts from investments in social initiatives. A good example can be seen with diversity and inclusion. While it is proven that diversity helps accelerate innovation and engagement, this positive impact can take years to demonstrate in an organization.

Until sustainable finance is more widely adopted and different performance metrics are recognized by financial systems, the current economic model will evolve slowly. Yet, the Positive Impact Marketer can accelerate this transformation of the system from within their organizations by driving SMART*i* goals and scorecards aimed at measuring short to long-term performance across all value dimensions. The marketer is in the best position to partner with all functions involved to ensure that assessments are thoroughly carried out across the entire value chain. The marketer can also ensure that value is measured and captured in a holistic way looking beyond financial and short-term value, and can prioritize actions toward quick wins that will demonstrate value creation on all these aspects.

Leadership skills for tomorrow

The next roadblock to the evolution of sustainable business is related to leadership styles and the skill set of today's leaders. As business models and the economic system evolve, so must leadership. Yesterday's leaders were rewarded for profit creation and expertise in each industry or field. Today, a new set of leadership qualities will be required to lead a company through the transformation of becoming successful and sustainably responsible. We have clearly seen an evolution towards recognizing the importance of soft skills in leaders.

Jim Collins proposed in the early 2000s the concept of the Level 5 Leader in his book *Good to Great*. The Level 5 Leader promotes leadership qualities that "build greatness through combination of humility and professional will." The Level 5 Leader is the culmination of five levels of leadership, each progressively more effective than the previous level. The Level 1 Leader is the "highly capable individual." The Level 2 Leader is the "contributing team member" who is not only effective as an individual but also contributes to the effectiveness of a team. The Level 3 Leader is the "competent manager" who can organize people and resources in the pursuit of objectives. The Level 4 Leader is the "effective leader" who catalyzes commitment and leads the group to high performance.

Here are the key traits of the "level 5" Leader:

- Put success of their organization ahead of personal success,
- Can be shy but passionate about getting the job done,
- Have a vision for the future of the company and their successor,
- Modest, quick to credit others,
- Take responsibility in times of failure.

We can already see in this evolution the greater care for people, the future of the company, and the need for humility. These traits are essential for establishing sustainable businesses.

Another trend in leadership style emerged in the 1970s when Robert Greenleaf first introduced the concept of Servant Leadership. This concept has received renewed popularity more recently. A servant leader is committed to transforming the world for the better and to helping others. The Greenleaf Center for Servant Leadership defines servant leadership as "a philosophy and set of practices that enriches the lives of individuals, builds better organizations and ultimately creates a more just and caring world."

Servant Leadership creates sustainable and healthy organizations. Servant leaders put others' interests ahead of self-interest. Over time, employees will align with a shared purpose, vision, value system, and principles. In turn, it will be easier to reach organizational short- and long-term goals.

The key principles and values of Servant Leadership are:

- Build trust through listening and authenticity,
- Inspire teams with strong vision—the Why, What, and How,
- Demonstrate integrity and strong ethics,
- Show empathy and compassion for others,
- Empower teams with autonomy and permission to fail,
- Continuous improvement mindset balancing focus and flexibility,
- Serve with humility and put others first—Committed to the success of others.

This concept has given rise to the leadership styles we hear about today, such as regenerative leadership or positive leadership. What we see in common in these leadership concepts is care, humility, and respect for people. These are essential qualities for the leader of a sustainable positive impact business who must care about employees as well as external stakeholders and their environment. These humble, caring, and respectful leaders are able to take a holistic and systemic approach, positioning the business and company within its world. Today's leaders must care about people, the environment, and the planet in the short and long-term. Beyond being caring individuals, they also need to be even more visionary, audacious, and courageous than leaders used to be. Visionary to see what the world needs and how they can contribute. Audacious to set the ambitions for their organizations and partners. Courageous to tackle these ambitions and deliver deep change. If we are to move to action to conquer sustainability challenges, tomorrow's leaders should demonstrate a strong bias for transformative and collaborative action.

All these skills must complement and reinforce the more traditional skills such as integrity. Today's leaders must absolutely be able to create trust, which involves walking the talk, doing what they say, and being honest and precise with their claims. In parallel, skills such as agility, adaptability, and resilience also become even more critical.

There is a great similarity in how the competences of the Positive Impact Marketer must evolve as for any leader. We'll cover that in the final section.

The "fear" syndrome

The final roadblock I would like to expand on is one that seems to emerge nowadays in parallel to stronger and stronger alarming messages.

Transformation can take place because of different forces. There can be a sudden change or crisis followed by a revolution, or situations may evolve and develop over time. Although we are experiencing an increase in environmental and social crises, these have not yet led to a revolution upending our economic system. The more and more devastating climate-related catastrophic events or the COVID-19 pandemic or the Ukraine-Russia war are all events that help accelerate the evolution of our economic system.

Citizens and consumers are becoming more aware and inclined to act and companies are also taking more actions towards sustainability. The creation of a Chief Sustainability Officer (CSO) position and establishment of Corporate Social Responsibility (CSR) programs were seen as highly progressive initiatives ten years ago. Today, developing a CSR program and appointing an executive to lead it are commonplace. Companies are publishing more and more thorough non-financial reports. Change is taking place, but gradually.

The most recent IPPC reports and planetary boundaries analysis strongly suggest that we need to accelerate the transformation. Despite this need for action, with the multiplication of crises and alarming messages, we see an underlying trend that is countering the necessary evolution; that trend is *fear*.

Fear is perceived firstly at the individual level. The repeated messages around the climate crisis while necessary for accelerating evolution also create a counter effect of denial and rejection. This leads to an increase of anxiety and negative attitudes. While such attitudes are human nature and probably justified, they can paralyze and derail progress. Change and innovation require a positive attitude and confidence that solutions can be found, sentiments that are not favored by fear and hesitation. The same fear can be perceived at the company level. Companies can be apprehensive about doing something in the right direction for fear of being accused of greenwashing or "not doing enough." This second-guessing is not productive: the task at hand is so huge that one must start somewhere. Making a change sustainable requires a step-by-step evolution. While it is important to ensure companies are not misleading through greenwashing, it is also important to support transformation efforts when they are genuine. "We can't eat the elephant in one bite," as the saying goes. Likewise, we must accept that deep transformations take time. As mentioned earlier, these transformations are certainly more complex for large companies and in particular those that have based their business model on nonsustainable resources. Yet if we want the economic system to be transformed, we need these large companies that represent a big pillar of our economy to transform.

Thus, what is important is *progress* in terms of positive impact. If there were ever a reason to add another "P" to the 3 Pillars of sustainable development, this would be it: People, Planet, Profit, and *Progress*. While accelerating progress toward the sustainable development goals is key, it is also reassuring for all that need to move to action. That is, progress helps diminish fear and creates the much-needed confidence to take action. While we need "moonshots" to accelerate any transformation, these need to be inspiring, positive, but also achievable.

As this transition continues, it is within the control of the Positive Impact Marketer to accelerate the transformation of our economic system with an authentic marketing plan that sets clear milestones to show progress over time. The Positive Impact Marketer, while pursuing SMART*i* goals, will be able to show and measure progress. Prioritizing activities toward greater value creation is a fundamental role of the marketer. When considering all aspects of value creation—economic, environmental, and social—the Positive Impact Marketer can have a huge impact on accelerating these transformations through concrete steps.

The evolving role of the CMO

Hopefully, the **Connect 4 Impact** methodology has provided the necessary toolbox for business leaders and marketers to establish sustainable business models. Yet, as explained earlier, Positive Impact Marketing requires a different mindset. To enable this mindset, the role of the CMO must also evolve (Figure 7.1).

Considering how businesses must evolve and the pivotal role of Positive Impact Marketing, can any business afford not to have marketing represented on the executive team of the company? The Chief Marketing Officer (CMO) who adopts the **Connect 4 Impact** approach can create the necessary link between all parts of the business internally and position it in its environment both in space and time. This "seat at the

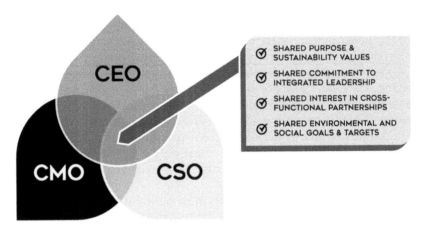

SHARED PURPOSE & SUSTAINABILITY VALUES

SHARED COMMITMENT TO INTEGRATED LEADERSHIP

SHARED INTEREST IN CROSS-FUNCTIONAL PARTNERSHIPS

SHARED ENVIRONMENTAL AND SOCIAL GOALS & TARGETS

Figure 7.1 The evolving role of the CMO.

table" for marketing is particularly critical for a sustainable business as it can strengthen the required partnerships within the company.

A partner to the CSO

As explained earlier, the mission of the Positive Impact Marketer is to establish sustainable business models. As such, the CMO, driven by Positive Impact Marketing, shares the same objectives as the CSO and are de facto natural partners.

Beyond sharing the same mission, they also share the same beliefs toward the value of partnerships and systemic approaches.

The CSO is key for the sustainability transformation of the company and has a pivotal role to play in understanding what should be done, and in measuring and tracking progress. Yet, when it comes to truly transforming the company at the level of its business models, the CSO must engage all functions within the organization. The objective of the CSO is to make sure that sustainability is embedded in all parts of the business as well as within the company strategy. Thus, partnering with the CMO in Positive Impact Marketing will be critical to ensure that sustainability is at the core of the business model.

In addition, the CSO and the CMO will see great benefits in partnering as they perform their respective roles. As we have seen in the **Connect 4 Impact** methodology, the traditional tools of marketing must be used in conjunction with the CSR tools to ensure the necessary focus on social and environmental issues. A key example of this use of traditional tools is the analysis of the business environment. It's the job of the Positive Impact Marketer to understand the entire ecosystem and the externalities of the business and to map the stakeholders. Likewise, the CSO looks to do this at a company level and define priorities for its transformation. The materiality analysis and matrix mentioned in the ecosystem analysis performed by the Positive Impact Marketer is a tool developed for the use of the CSO to define the sustainability strategy. Thus, for the CMO to make sure the stakeholder mapping and ecosystem mapping is comprehensive, collaboration with the CSO is essential.

Another example of the value of partnership between the CMO and the CSO is a shared interest in impact assessment and measurement. To ensure the impact measurement is done reliably, with the transparency and consistency required, collaboration is needed. As mentioned earlier, to build credibility, a company must work with an appropriate and recognized measurement and certification entity and must be consistent over time. These are objectives shared by the CSO and CMO.

Finally, as we look to establish new business models and paradigm shifts, there is always a component of change management. Influential leadership is important to the CMO and CSO, and as they share the same objectives, they can only be stronger together. This partnership will enable a combined focus on the "What" as well as on the "How" of the transformation that will make the change easier to accept and implement across the company.

A partner to the CEO

Beyond personal belief, there are many reasons why a CEO should want to engage in a CSR strategy. From an employee perspective, a CSR strategy helps attract and retain talent as more employees look for a sense of purpose in their jobs. From a business continuity perspective, a CSR strategy will help mitigate risk, reduce costs, and increase business resilience. From an image perspective, it will strengthen the corporate reputation and brand. Finally, from an innovation perspective, sustainability, as demonstrated earlier in the book, is the source for endless innovation opportunities. These examples are just a few of the benefits of a CSR strategy for a company. All these opportunities—employee satisfaction, continuity, reputation, and innovation—reinforce the importance of the CEO and the CMO operating in partnership to establish sustainability in the business model and the company overall.

Let's take the example of corporate reputation. As explained earlier, it is critical for Positive Impact Marketing to establish credibility. This comes through consistency in action over time and consistency between claims and actions (walking the talk). For that reason, Positive Impact

Marketing cannot be done in isolation and must be fully coherent with the company's strategy, actions, and claims. This implies not only full alignment but an interdependency between marketing strategies and the company's strategy.

As companies are looking to either be impact businesses or transform themselves to become sustainable businesses, they must fully embed sustainability in the company's strategy. Positive Impact Marketing has a key role to play in fully embedding sustainability into each product/service strategy and hence into the company's strategy.

The positive impact chief marketer will also be the one that guarantees the sustainability of the business models and thus of the company.

In sum, the CMO must be a close partner to the CEO in any positive impact business—or those striving to be positive impact businesses.

Key competences of today's CMO

With the evolution of marketing as described in this book, the competences of the CMO need to evolve.

In the past, marketers had to have a good strategic mind, strong business acumen, and communication skills. They had to be creative as well as possessing market knowledge and technical competencies in marketing practices and tools. In the world of sustainability, soft skills are increasingly vital elements of the CMO skill set.

These soft skills include:

- **System thinking**
  First from the strategic point of view, the Positive Impact Marketer should have the ability to see things from a broader perspective and connect all the dots—that is, the Positive Impact Marketer is able to take a systemic look at a given environment and not only perceive the dots but integrate all the parts with a solution-oriented mindset.

- **Inclusive and collaborative**
  Then, to form the partnerships needed for systemic approaches, the marketer should have the ability to see things from different perspectives, to apprehend and respect different ways of thinking. Being inclusive is key to this new marketer. Possessing the ability to form meaningful partnerships and positive collaboration is also essential. Having an inclusive and collaborative mindset will be critical to the role.

- **Care for people and planet**
  Finally, a deep caring for the environment and for people is necessary. It is only when these are part of the values system of individuals and

embedded into who they are that they can consistently and genuinely bring the expected positive impact.

One can certainly draw a parallel between the skills of the CMO and the skills needed for the CSO or for tomorrow's leaders in general.

The great news is that education is evolving. Leadership courses have evolved and present new styles of leadership. We also see more and more executive education on leadership with purpose and happiness in the workplace where happiness is closely related to social and environmental considerations. In addition, from primary school onwards, we see more and more teaching related to sensitizing the students about sustainability challenges and positive impact. For today's leaders, specialized executive courses and master's programs are being developed to build knowledge and equip leaders to transform the economic system towards a more sustainable one. Finally, we see a promising trend to include sustainability concepts in each of the classes and not as a course on the side. These are all important evolutions in the education system to better equip the leaders we need today for tomorrow.

 Testimony

Defeating short-termism to achieve long-term, pragmatic solutions

Andrew Liveris—Former Chairman and CEO Dow Chemical, President Brisbane 2032 Olympic and Paralympic Games Organizing Committee, Director of Lucid Motors, IBM, Aramco, Worley, Novonix

I grew up in the outback of Australia, where the environment is pristine, the air is clean, and everything is like it should be. It's the most natural beauty in the world so I really care for the ecosystem that we all live in as humans. And I saw very early in my formative years at Dow the same awareness, at the most senior levels, of the importance of sustainability for the future of humanity, and the role that Dow could play. For example, when I was a middle manager, I noticed that Dow was one of the first companies to come forward and contribute to the triple bottom line, which was a novel concept at the time put in place by President Clinton. He appointed a Sustainability Council, and the chair of that Council was the Dow CEO, Frank Popoff.

When I became CEO in 2004, it was obvious to me that sustainability had to be an integral part of our business strategy. Back in the 90s Dow launched its "Footprint" goals and its first set of ten-year sustainability goals focusing on assets. A decade later, Footprint grew into "Handprint" anchored in our assets *and* our products. These weren't just slogans but embedded deeply in our vision and strategy. In 2009, I added a new value to Dow, which was "protecting our planet." and I said that going forward every product strategy, every business strategy now should have sustainability as its core driver. By 2011 we added "Blueprint" goals, addressing needs for society and the planet in this century as our license to operate.

Despite this long history of sustainability-driven strategy and focus, Dow is viewed as a bad actor by many. One reason is that in our ADD social media world and news based on opinions and not facts, you can't really present your case and be believed. Society listens to the celebrity culture, not to the people who have the facts, and have the long-term perspective to promote pragmatic, achievable solutions.

It's not just the media. The way the world is constructed, our politicians and our financial managers are also fixated on the short term. That's why I believe short-termism is the number one systemic roadblock to achieving the long-term, managed solutions we need. A second roadblock, which feeds into short-termism, is education. The 21st century needs a different type of education system, which is why I started the Academy at my university, the University of Queensland, to train undergraduate students to actually understand how to make content and context decisions—so they do not get labeled but build their label. And finally, the rhetoric of Wokeism, based on the belief that it can only be one way or another, there is no compromise—that has people running away from doing the right things environmentally, socially, and through governance (ESG is now seen as a bad acronym!) is another roadblock.

Overcoming these roadblocks begins with a bottom-up approach, through which community-based groups—companies, NGOs, academia, or any part of the system that is community-based—put forward long-term, practical solutions that promote inclusive capitalism, meaning a system that is inclusive of all stakeholders. We also need to protect the CEOs who believe that purpose-based business is profitable from shareholder activists unhappy that they are not making short-term profits. And we need enlightened board members who come from different sectors and from different groups. The European model of a supervisory board, which includes different representatives of the ecosystem and the value chain, comes to mind.

For any leader who wants to be engaged in creating the systemic change we need, I would say first, lean into what can be done, lean into the art of the possible versus being a passive resistor to the seemingly impossible. Second, do the hard work; learn the content, but work hard on the context of every decision you make. You need to have the *depth* to be a subject-matter expert, but also the *width* to understand all the adjacencies. Finally, I would say embrace the reality versus imagining the fantasy. Create and make a conscious choice to implement a plan A. If you're wrong, pivot quickly to a plan B and plan C.

One final word about marketing specifically. The rate of change of all these disruptions—which I describe along with leadership recommendations for dealing with them in my 2023 book, *Leading through Disruption*—is so tremendous that the old way of thinking of marketing has to be reinvented. In the last century, we had consumer marketing and industrial marketing, which is unfortunately still being taught, and it is completely wrong. We are not paying attention to the reinvention of markets and the paradigm shift in how to approach these markets—think Amazon, think Tesla. For example, at Lucid, the EV company I'm part of, we have a product but what we've realized is we're selling a holistic experience, engaging the customer.

Bibliography

James C. Collins. *Good to Great.* Harper Collins, 2001.
Robert K. Greenleaf. *Servant Leadership: A Journey into the Nature of Legitimate Power and Greatness.* 25th Anniversary Edition. Paulist Press, 2012.
Andrew Liveris. *Leading through Disruption.* Harper Collins Leadership, 2023.

Conclusion

A new mindset for marketing

Today, I am very hopeful that we are going in the right direction. Yet, when looking at the increasing number of crises related to climate change and social imbalances, we definitely need to accelerate the switch from *talking* about the challenges to *acting* on them. The intention of this book is to provide a toolkit for today's and tomorrow's business leaders to take action that will lead to the transformation of our economic model, which is a must for the sustainable development of our planet and people.

Beyond a framework to complement traditional practices, the transformation requires an evolution in mindset. As demonstrated in the book, marketing, which has always been there to serve businesses, must now evolve with the evolving role of business in society. As such, marketing can now extend its purpose to serve today's and tomorrow's people and planet needs. If used in line with its roots and complemented with some of the key corporate social responsibility tools, it can help businesses undergo a deep transformation. One that touches the business model and can be sustained over time. One that would help establish sustainability in business.

For this, we need a new mindset for marketing. Based on the key takeaways of this book and to summarize its core concept, I would describe the new mindset for marketing in the following key points.

- Forge a sustainability mindset and develop an understanding of why and how the role of business needs to evolve toward positive impact businesses,
- Be true to the original intentions of marketing going back to basics,
- Get familiar with the Corporate Social Responsibility (CSR) transformation tools: SDGs, ecosystem analysis, planetary boundaries, Materiality Matrix ...,
- Adopt a system-thinking mindset to understand the externalities of your business and your positive and negative impact on all stakeholders and across the entire life cycle,

DOI: 10.4324/9781003422709-9

- Take a collaborative approach looking for impactful partnerships,
- Demonstrate care in targeting unmet needs that serve the planet and society and develop objectives for your marketing strategy and marketing mix that address the three pillars of sustainability: People, Planet, Profit,
- Be transparent and honest in measuring impact,
- Build trust and ensure consistency between say and do as well as across the company,
- Be a champion for transverse corporate approaches and partner with all functions in the organization to align objectives and actions,
- Be bold in setting ambitious yet realistic sustainability-driven objectives.

I would like to conclude this book by referring to one of these influential leaders who is opening new fronts in the campaign for sustainability. As we think about the role of business in society, the oriental culture provides new horizons that could inspire the necessary mindset for sustainability to be embedded not only in business but in our way of living and interacting with our environment at large. The fourth king of Bhutan introduced in the early 1970s the concept of "Gross National Happiness," which is now supported by an index itself instituted as the goal of the government of Bhutan in the Constitution of Bhutan. The concept implies that sustainable development should take a holistic approach toward notions of progress and give equal importance to non-economic aspects of well-being. This leads the way to a new economic paradigm where value is redefined based on collective happiness and the well-being of a population.

About the author

Clara Millard Dereudre is a pragmatic visionary. A farmer's daughter with her feet firmly on the ground yet exposed in her career to many different industries and different regions of the world, she is driven by the challenges of a sustainable development (in their broadest sense, whether human, social, environmental, or economic) and, above all, the search for solutions. As a mother of two teenage girls, Clara wants to contribute to a sustainable world for the next generations. She is particularly committed to the role that companies can and must play in addressing these issues.

Clara has extensive experience in managing industrial profit centers, developing, and implementing transformation strategies as well as managing large multidisciplinary and multicultural teams. She worked with Dow Chemical for 25 years, holding different leadership positions in sales, marketing, innovation, strategy, and sustainability. During those 25 years, sustainable development challenges became prominent across industries and geographies. In her last role as Sr Global Marketing, Strategy and Sustainability Director for the $5 billion Industrial Solutions business, Clara was appointed Sr Corporate Marketing Fellow. As such, she joined the global corporate commercial management team, championing how marketing could help position sustainability at the core of business strategies.

In early 2021, Clara was appointed Executive Director of Smart City and a member of the general management team with SIG—Industrial Services of Geneva, an independent public sector company providing utilities (energy, water, telecommunication, waste management, electric mobility) and committed to a sustainable and connected society.

A graduate of EDHEC (MSc in Business Management) in France and with an MBA from Northwood University in Michigan, USA, she lives and leads by strong ethical standards and is an ambassador for the role of business in society. Clara is an MBA/MSc visiting professor in Sustainability Marketing teaching sustainable marketing and management. She is a member of boards of directors (FONGIT Innovation Hub

DOI: 10.4324/9781003422709-10

Geneva, HEG Business School Geneva, Smart Data Energy, Luminotechnique SA and SBB CFF FFS - Swiss Federal Railways) and is involved in a number of civic and associative activities to further sustainable development. Clara founded the association Greenbuzz Geneva, whose aim is to enable the exchange of best practices and collaboration between leaders in sustainable development.

Index

Milton Keynes UK
Ingram Content Group UK Ltd.
UKHW021623041224
451949UK00025B/464